CHILDHOOD TRAUMA
AND THE NON-ALPHA MALE

Gender Role Conflict, Toxic Shame and Complex Trauma:
Finding Hope, Clarity, Healing and Change

DOUGLAS W. CARPENTER, Psy.D.

PRAISE FOR
CHILDHOOD TRAUMA AND THE NON-ALPHA MALE

With great compassion, Doug Carpenter challenges the reader to assess their own biases and behaviors related to gender beliefs, toxic shame, and complex trauma. In doing so, he leads us all to a world of far greater safety and authentic vulnerability — a world of love, acceptance and kindness for ourselves and others. *[Childhood Trauma]* is an important book whose time is overdue.

– Claudia Black, author of *Unspoken Legacy: Addressing the Impact of Trauma and Addiction Within the Family*

"There is a dearth of books written focused on men and psychology; however, more and more attention is being paid to this necessary area of study. Doug Carpenter has added to this growing area of interest by providing a thoughtful exploration of a very important topic: men and childhood trauma. Men's trauma is often very invisible to them and their loved ones while the impact of that trauma can tear their lives apart. Grounded in research while using a heartbreaking case study to amplify and support his points, Carpenter makes the argument that men who struggle to fit into the dominant masculine identity have a unique experience of trauma that follows them long into their lives and yet, healing is possible."

– Dan Griffin, MA author of *A Man's Way through Relationships: Learning to Love and Be Loved*

Dr. Carpenter has done it again! This book is both timely and authoritative on the topic of male gender identity formation. He is a true professor in every sense of the word, and his current work allows the reader to digest the topic of complex trauma as it relates to the formation of male gender identify on an academic, professional, and deeper personal level. Dr. Carpenter's critical review of research, examples from over 20 years of clinical experience, and his pushing of the reader to personally reflect pulls the topic together in a masterful way!

> — Bowman Smelko, Psy.D ABPP, Licensed Psychologist
> Board Certified in Forensic Psychology

This book offers a profound viewpoint of the delicate development of gender identity and entices the reader to ponder the stereotype of males and a family and society's role in perpetuating that typecast. It challenges the engrained view of masculinity and potential damages of holding on to these archaic views. Definitely a worthwhile read.

> — Annie Beattie-Powers, Licensed Psychologist

This book is timely and full of hope and restoration for anyone seeking to heal from toxic shame. The self-reflection questions at the end of each chapter provide opportunity for further insight. Dr. Douglas Carpenter is a master at unraveling the complex relationship between toxic shame, trauma and gender role conflict.

> — Debbie Walker, PsyD., Licensed Psychologist
> Coordinator, Southwest Baptist University
> Counseling Services

Dr. Carpenter addresses the confusion and isolation felt by so many men in today's society. With thorough and compassionate exploration, packed with essential empirical research, Dr. Carpenter has created a path guiding men to understanding and accepting their core self. I highly recommend this book to both families and clinicians as this is truly a valuable resource.

Dr. Carpenter's book on childhood trauma serves as a great resource! This book is beneficial for any individual who strives to have a deeper understanding of gender roles and guidance on how to dismantle toxic shame and complex trauma and promote healthy gender development. He has crafted an informative book with guided self-reflection and real-world examples.

Dr. Carpenter created an excellent resource for all new and seasoned therapists. His integration of current and past research, prominent authors, and 20+ years of working with male trauma survivors is a must read for patients as well. He takes the reader on a journey from birth to adulthood and explores interpersonal challenges, developmental issues, and relationship dynamics of abuse survivors. He then offers the reader reflective statements and therapeutic "talking points" to use with all patients. Overall, it is an excellent contribution to the field and allows generalization for therapeutic providers from a Cognitive Behavioral to a completely interpersonal or psychodynamic orientation.

Childhood Trauma and the Non-Alpha Male
Gender Role Conflict, Toxic Shame, and Complex Trauma:
Finding Hope, Clarity, Healing, and Change

Library of Congress Cataloging-in-Publication Data

Names: Carpenter, Douglas W., author.
Title: Childhood trauma and the non-alpha male/gender role conflict, toxic
    shame, and complex trauma : finding hope, clarity, healing, and change /
    Douglas W. Carpenter, Psy.D.
Description: Ocala, Florida : Atlantic Publishing Group, Inc., [2018] |
    Includes bibliographical references and index.
Identifiers: LCCN 2018018960 (print) | LCCN 2018020348 (ebook) | ISBN
    9781620235997 (ebook) | ISBN 9781620235980 (alk. paper)
Subjects: LCSH: Masculinity. | Gender identity. | Sex role--Psychological
    aspects. | Psychic trauma in children.
Classification: LCC BF692.5 (ebook) | LCC BF692.5 .C377 2018 (print) | DDC
    155.3/32--dc23
LC record available at https://lccn.loc.gov/2018018960

Over the years, we have adopted a number of dogs from rescues and shelters. First there was Bear and after he passed, Ginger and Scout. Now, we have Kira, another rescue. They have brought immense joy and love not just into our lives, but into the lives of all who met them.

We want you to know a portion of the profits of this book will be donated in Bear, Ginger and Scout's memory to local animal shelters, parks, conservation organizations, and other individuals and nonprofit organizations in need of assistance.

*— **Douglas & Sherri Brown**,*
President & Vice-President of Atlantic Publishing

DEDICATION

To my dear parents for the
life they have given me;
to my wife for her unconditional love
and acceptance;
and to my children,
Dawson and Morgan

You are the loves of my life.

ACKNOWLEDGEMENTS

To my parents, I thank you for many years of parenting from infancy into adulthood. I treasure the values and morals you instilled in me from an early age. You are both a consistent source of support and strength in my life. I also am deeply indebted to my wife and children, who patiently allowed time for me to complete this work, listened to my ideas, and provided valuable feedback. I love you dearly. Thank you to my friend and colleague, Diana Andre, for your editing, creativity, and advice. You are truly a brainchild! I would also like to thank Atlantic Publishing and my editor, Katie Cline, for her hours of work, suggestions, and insights.

I want to acknowledge and thank all my patients who have struggled with the issues of trauma, toxic shame, and gender role conflict. Your bravery and willingness to seek healing are an inspiration for many, and this book could not have been compiled without you sharing your experiences. I am grateful for each one of you, and I pray for continued healing and strength throughout your journey.

Lastly and above all, I thank God for his careful guidance and healing along life's journey. I can do all things through Him, who strengthens me.

TABLE OF CONTENTS

FOREWORD

Gender role conflict is a powerful force that leads men down many roads, some through pain and heartache, and others through great joy and excitement. In the pages of this book you will read how many males, and specifically how one young man, struggled with his gifts, talents, personality, and even his state of being.

As the author, I write of individuals' experiences, along with related research, as a framework to help others understand the vital aspects of maturation as it relates to gender role conflict, toxic shame, complex trauma, and ultimately, gender identity development for boys and men. Compared to research of females, empirical studies of males regarding gender role conflict, shame, types of abuse, and specifically the sexual abuse of boys, by both male and female perpetrators, is significantly inefficient. Over many decades of research, the emotional development and tragedy of male development and trauma has taken a back seat to the experiences of females. Unfortunately, the clinical community has fallen prey to society's trap of believing that females are more emotional by nature and more easily harmed by physical and emotional turmoil.

This book is an examination of how early gender role conflict can lead to complex trauma; how resulting toxic shame can distort a child's self-perception; how subsequent bullying can impact a child's life; and, most importantly, how these obstacles can be mitigated and overcome by boys and men.

Although no two stories are the same, each of us develops our sense of purpose through our unique set of challenges and the resulting triumphs and defeats. My clients have worked to find their self-worth, purpose, and acceptance through a difficult process of suffering and struggling — they have fought through complex trauma and toxic shame to peel back layers of degradation and free themselves from mental bondage. You may be unfamiliar with the terms 'complex trauma' and 'toxic shame'; these will be defined. I am excited to now share their journeys with you.

As illustrated through a detailed account of Ben's life, we will examine how a parent's personal upbringing can dramatically impact how they guide and parent their own children. A common result is that parents attempt to overcompensate when rearing their own children by doing the exact opposite of what their parents did to try and help their child avoid the pain they themselves experienced. While this is a noble attempt at correction, it is often as damaging as the original course.

Effective parenting requires one to strike a balance between defining and avoiding the mistakes inherent in one's own upbringing, resisting overcompensation, understanding the unique needs of your child, and modeling a life of moderation. I am a strong supporter of Pia Melody RN, ABCAC, and Claudia Black Ph.D., who convincingly argue parents must function in a realm of moderation to allow healthy child development. You will see many references throughout this book to Pia Melody's and Claudia Black's work. Granted, finding balance and trying to rear children is a challenge, but it is well worth the effort and dedication.

The names presented in the book are fictitious and stories have been altered, as I have tried to conceal the identity of anyone mentioned to respect their privacy and their own story. Healing is not about blame; it is about finding your voice, fostering forgiveness, and arriving at acceptance. It requires you to examine the facts, the impact of those events, work through them in a constructive manner, and recalibrate your life accordingly. *Experience Hope, Healing, Clarity, and Change* is the tagline for Insight Counseling Services, my personal counseling practice. These steps are my personal goals, as well as the goals for the patients I work with on a daily basis.

As you read these pages, I encourage you to reflect on your own experience, your adherence to your masculine or feminine ideology, how your life events have impacted you, and how you can mitigate the harmful impact any of these events may have had. I believe you also can experience *Hope, Healing, Clarity, and Change.*

01 | THE PARENT CALLING

"There are only two lasting bequests
we can hope to give our children.
One of these is roots, the other, wings."

— Johann Wolfgang von Goethe

The birth of a child is an amazing miracle to witness. Life unfolds before your eyes and suddenly you're holding a miniature you! Immediately, an overwhelming feeling of responsibility washes over you with the force of a fast-flowing river. How can you comprehend that you are responsible for this small life?

Maslow's Hierarchy of Needs has now become a reality in this bundle of joy you hold in your arms. You realize you are responsible for the basic needs of food, water, clothing, and safety, as well as providing love and giving this child a secure attachment to a caregiver who will fulfill his or her need of belonging. You must give all your effort for this child to develop the components necessary to become a self-actualized adult. Are you feeling overwhelmed yet?

Developmental Psychology

Developmental psychology is a broad and expansive area of study. Many theorists, researchers, clinicians, and authors have offered roadmaps to help parents understand the great responsibility of raising children. One such author is Claudia Black, Ph.D. In her book, *Changing Course: Healing from Loss, Abandonment, and Fear*, she proposes the idea that a child is born with a "Bill of Rights". She postulates every child has the right:

- to be loved for who he or she is, rather than for being what others wish him or her to become;
- to be nurtured and parented, rather than to make up for the parents' losses;
- to have consistency, security, warmth, and understanding; and
- to be protected from traumatic situations.

Black uses these concepts to demonstrate that children are dependent on those to whom they are entrusted. The parent must work to nurture a safe environment where the individual will receive the positive attention and adequate care required. If children lack these basic given rights while they're developing, they will grow up feeling unsafe in the world. Eventually, the result will be the emergence of an unhealthy lifestyle in regards to their relationships with self and others.[1]

---

1 Black, 1993

Pia Melody, RN, in her book *Facing Codependency*, discusses the nature of a child and contends,

> When children are born, they have five natural characteristics that make them authentic human beings: children are valuable, vulnerable, imperfect, dependent, and immature. All children are born with these attributes. Functional parents help their children to develop each separate characteristic properly, so they arrive in adulthood as mature, functional adults who feel good about themselves.[2]

These five concepts are important to examine individually.

Valuable

Children are born valuable. He or she is born equal to others and does not need to earn his or her inherent worth as a person. Children need to be loved and told they are of value because they are; they exist, they were created, they were born! This requires the parent to devote ample time and attention to the child in order to confirm his or her worth.

Vulnerable and imperfect

As parents, we must remember children are vulnerable: they are born defenseless and deserve protection on all levels. They cannot defend themselves from physical or emotional harm. It is our responsibility, as parents, to guard against potential dangers. It is a balancing act to appropriately protect children without smothering or coddling.

The famous words of the philosopher John Locke, *"tabula rasa"*, are applicable to the nature of imperfection; children are born as "blank

---

2   Melody, 1989

slates". They lack knowledge and do not yet know how to problem-solve. Children learn primarily by being taught when an adult writes on the blank slate and imparts knowledge to the child. Therefore, adults must expect for children to be imperfect and to make frequent mistakes. Children must be given the opportunity to explore their world and feel the freedom to make mistakes, without the fear of being shamed and ridiculed for not yet possessing the full abilities and comprehension of adults. Developing children are imperfect: they experiment, they react to stimuli, and they are spontaneous.

Dependent

Children are born dependent and have needs before they also quickly develop wants. It remains the parents' responsibility to supply those needs accordingly, and to supply children their wants in an appropriate manner. It is vital to assist children in discriminating between needs and wants, as well as teach them how to properly prioritize each.

Jarek is an active 2-year-old who suffers with Diabetes Insipidus, a condition in which the kidneys do not hold water and results in frequent, heavy urination and unquenchable thirst. Due to his condition, Jarek requires a diaper change every 30 to 45 minutes. Unfortunately, Jarek tends to suffer from severe diaper rash because his mother refuses to change his diaper as required and yells at him stating she "will only change his diaper every two hours." His mother chronically complains that he "is simply too demanding." Additionally, she refuses to fill his drink cup as much as he wants and shames him for having so many constant requests. Jarek has the potential to develop a host of problems as a result of his mother's denial to meet his needs and wants, including, but not limited to the:

- inability to live a life of moderation;

- demand that his needs/wants are met immediately
  and instantly;
- requirement that others care for him;
- need for the constant attention of others;
- difficulty controlling his emotions;
- belief that no one will ever listen to him;
- self-denial of his own needs and wants;
- development of a co-dependent mindset in which he works
  to meet the needs of others to the detriment and dismissal
  of his own.

As seen in Jarek's case, children must not be shamed for their needs or wants. When children have a need, it is the parent's responsibility to supply it and not push them away, nor offer excuses for not supplying the need.

Immature/spontaneous

Children are immature and spontaneous and should be allowed to explore their environment, learning to balance work and fun. A schedule and structure is important in the developing life of a child, but rigidity and a lack of spontaneity can be harmful. Children can learn to live within the boundaries of a healthy schedule while still being spontaneous in their play, interaction, and activity.

A quote from French psychiatrist Pierre Janet reads, "Every life is a piece of art put together with all means available." Children need all the necessary components to develop into healthy, functional adults. What happens when these necessary parts are not provided or the child is born into ready-made, pre-set expectations while the parents ignore the child's own unique set of needs and desires?

CASE EXAMPLE

An example in which parents failed to recognize their child's own uniqueness and abilities can be found in the life of Marcus. His father moved to the United States to improve his family's quality of life and escape the tyranny in his home country. He had been a physician, working long hours to establish himself as a successful doctor in the United States. Marcus' father felt being a physician was the only way to advance in this new country and create wealth. A few years after coming to the states, Marcus was born. Before even entering the world, there was a great expectation that Marcus would grow up to become a physician like his dad. The father vowed his family and future generations would never suffer the poverty they had endured in their homeland. Marcus was told since he was a toddler what was expected of him in school, in his studies, and ultimately, in medical school; he was never given a choice. As Marcus grew, he did not particularly care for the medical field but knew his father's wishes took priority. He graduated high school and went on to college to study pre-medicine. After five years of undergraduate work, Marcus sits in my office severely depressed, anxious, and isolated. He feels lost and overwhelmed by expectations and family-imposed guilt. Marcus has struggled with many classes throughout his college career and knows he is not meant for the medical field. He is now faced with the challenge of defying his father by seeking his own personal and professional goals.

The psychological damage Marcus has endured cannot be understood if taken only at face value. He has deep emotional wounds from disappointing his father and believes he is letting down his family. His depression stems from the denial of his own desires and from not having a positive sense of personal identity. He is anxious around his peers and is fearful in social settings. Marcus has never learned to trust and rely on his own feelings because his life was always planned for him; his own desires had been belittled and discarded.

An upbringing devoid of individualized respect and care can be damaging to the psyche of a child. The child, as a result, doubts his or her worth and abilities, and these doubts induce shame, acting as a megaphone in the mind of the child, blasting messages of negativity. The natural rights of this child have been violated and they have been robbed of the chance to develop into a complete and autonomous person.

"Less-Than Messages"

Pia Melody writes,

> Children learn self-esteem first from their major caregivers. But dysfunctional caregivers give their children, verbally or nonverbally, the message that the children are 'less-than' people. These "less-than" messages from the caregivers become part of the children's own opinions of themselves. Upon reaching adulthood, it is almost impossible for those raised with 'less-than' messages to be able to generate the feeling from within that they have value.

She also writes, "I believe the worst experience for children is to have their reality denied."[3] The reality is that every child deserves to be loved, simply because they are — they exist; they are a human in need of nurturance.

---

3   Melody, 1989

No matter what theory of parenting you decide to follow, it is important to recognize the magnitude and immense obligation of your role as a parent. You have been entrusted with the responsibility of guiding an innocent child's life and being the primary author upon his or her blank slate. They are molding clay — your words, your behavior, your decisions, your example mold them. Your words will become their inner voice. Remember that!

SELF-REFLECTION QUESTIONS

1. *What do you believe are a child's rights?*

2. *What are your thoughts about the true nature of a child in response to Claudia Black and Pia Melody?*

3. *What is some of the information written on your blank slate before the age of 5?*

4. *Were there expectations placed on you as a child that you feel were unfair?*

5. *What "less-than" messages play in your head on a mega-phone?*

02

CONVERGENCE OF SEX AND GENDER

"Talk with your children and you will hear their voice. Walk with them through life and you will feel their heart"

— Geoff Resse

The role of a parent begins before birth. Typically, around 20 weeks of gestation, the expectant mother has a sonogram to learn the biological sex of the child. Excitement abounds as sonogram pictures are posted on Facebook and Instagram, party plans are made, and the world is quickly informed of the child's sex before he or she has made their true, physical debut. As soon as expectant parents know the sex of their baby, they start planning the child's life accordingly: they paint the nursery to reflect the child's sex; shower invitations are color coordinated, and pink or blue gifts registered for; and even great-aunt

Gertrude rushes out to buy the right colors of yarn for the baby blanket she's waited to knit until the sex of the baby is made public. Seemingly, most parents do not consciously decide to raise a child to be either a boy or girl — it is the result of nature's sex determination, and parents' behaviors tend to follow accordingly.

There are many automatic, unconscious processes that occur as a result of finding out the child's sex. Most parents don't actively consider the implications of the toys or stuffed animals that will go in the infant's nursery, but lions, tigers, and trucks are bought for little boys, while cute, fluffy kitties, dolls, and tea sets are bought for little girls. Before they even emerge from the womb, the world is preparing to instill the child's gender, based solely upon their biological sex.

Even the chosen name for this new bundle of joy is driven by sex and gender. This name alone acts as a life-long roadmap telling people how to interact with them. As this infant matures, their given name, toys provided, and even the color of their clothes will all work harmoniously to give cues about their sex, and ultimately, their gender role. Naturally, parents use language that provides the child with important information. Dad comes home from work, grabs his young son, and begins tossing him up in the air while asking, "How's my big boy doing today?" or twirls his daughter around the foyer asking, "How's my beautiful, little princess?" At the risk of sounding stereotypical, I want you to consider how many messages, such as these, are constantly received by a child about their sex and gender. These perfunctory, casual messages, many of which are universal, unintentional and automatic, are processed and absorbed into the child's psyche, thereby shaping their identity. For the majority of people, these messages align harmoniously with their inner identity, and the process runs smoothly.

In spite of the long-running feminist movement, our society has not yet deviated much from traditional roles assigned to each gender. Take a look at advertising during a Saturday morning television special or in the ads in the Sunday paper. Consider an ad for the Easy Bake Oven. The picture depicts a young girl and her friends or her mother enjoying their baked goods. Do boys not bake? Aren't there numerous chefs around the world who are male? Can you imagine a mother having denied Wolfgang Puck or Gordon Ramsay the ability to learn to cook from a young age? The Easy Bake Oven is one example of many you can find on the store shelf that continues to restrict and reinforce archaic, stereotypical gender roles.

Though many advertisers are working to remove these delineations, boys are still frequently shown as more dominate, aggressive, able to endure pain, less emotional, and task-oriented, whereas girls are stereotyped as nurturing, socially-oriented, and emotionally expressive; boys play with toy guns and race cars, while girls like Barbies and dress-up. Typically, it is not until adolescence that boys and girls begin to challenge some of these stereotypes.

Some major department stores, such as Target, have worked to break down this barrier by removing the "Boys" and "Girls" toy aisles, inter-mixing the toy shelves. In a media announcement, Metro said that:

> "Target has announced that they're now dedicated to mak-ing their stores more gender neutral, after hundreds of people tweeted their dismay at their gendered toy aisles. From now on, certain aisles where recommendations by gender are, frankly, completely unnecessary, will no longer have gender-specific sig-nage. Clothing signs will remain the same, while toys, entertain-ment, and home will have gender neutral makeover." [4]

---

4   Scott, 2015

Though department stores can change the face of their stores to be more gender neutral, what is modeled at home will continue to have the greatest impact on gender identity in early childhood development. Numerous research studies have shown children are rewarded by their parents when they are found to be playing with properly sex-typed toys[5], and also found boys are punished more for deviations from sex-typed toys than girls are.[6] Consider the potential long-term psychological effects on a child that is punished for playing with cross-gender toys. Boys, when punished for playing with toys such as ovens or dolls, are sent negative messages about care, sensitivity, and nurturance. These boys will have stereotypical outlooks ingrained in them from their own childhood and, as a result, may face challenges when confronted with it in their own children later on in life. Perhaps they will hold the archaic belief that child rearing responsibilities are a "woman's job", while their role is primarily to have fun with the children. We must consider how the messages we send out to children about themselves, their gender, and the world around them form the foundations of a belief system and personal identity that will last a lifetime.

Gender Research and Masculine Ideology

One of the paramount researchers in the area of gender is Joseph Pleck, Ph.D, a widely known author in the areas of fatherhood and masculinity who has spent a majority of his career studying gender ideology, masculinity, gender role identity, strain, and dysfunction. Throughout his works he has defined the concept of "masculinity ideology", referring to the beliefs about the importance of men adhering to culturally defined

---

5   Maccoby et al 1966, Steiner 1985, Houston 1983, & Ruble 1988
6   Blackemore, 2003

standards for male behaviors. He also proposes the definition for masculinity ideology can be different depending on various groups of men (e.g. civilian men compared to military men). Research concerning masculinity ideologies was being conducted as long ago as the 1950s and possibly before. These definitions can be diverse according to geography, social status, and culture.

The study of masculinity, gender, gender roles, sex roles, and various topics in these areas became more prevalent in the1960s and 1970s. Early works such as Eleanor Maccoby's *The Development of Sex Difference* (1966); John Money's and Anke Earhart's *Man and Woman, Boy and Girl* (1972); Eleanor Maccoby's & Carol Nagy Jackin's *The Psychology of Sex Differences* (1974); and Rhoda Kesler Unger's *Toward a Redefinition of Sex and Gender* (1979) brought these concepts into the forefront of research and introduced an era in which these important constructs were finally examined.

In her book, *Child Development* (2000), Laura Berk, Ph.D. defines gender roles as "the reflection of gender stereotypes in everyday behavior", and defines gender stereotypes as "widely-held beliefs about characteristics thought appropriate for males and females." She identified stereotypical masculine traits to be "active, aggressive, ambitious, competitive, dominant, superior, independent, and self-confident", whereas stereotypical feminine traits are "considerate, devotes self to others, emotional, gentle, home-oriented, kind, likes children, and passive." As the individual grows, each person will develop gender-related characteristics. Some individuals will either naturally, or via choice, align themselves with more traditional roles and actions. Others will develop a more idiosyncratic set of characteristics. Whatever characteristics emerge, each person begins to build a framework for their internal world and how they will choose to relate to the external world in relation to who they are and their gender identity. Consider these gender-specific trait preferences as you read the next several paragraphs, examining how a child develops their gender identity.

Gender Identity

In the world of Cognitive-Behavioral theory, we often use the word "schema", which can be thought of as an outline or a framework. Schemas develop from life experiences and information gathered, informing one about what to expect and how to think and behave in a given situation. Children develop a gender schema as soon as they begin to have an awareness of the differences between the genders.

Sandra Bem, Ph.D., one of the first psychologists to examine the concepts of androgyny and gender studies, has contributed greatly to the body of literature concerning gender schema theory. According to Dr. Bem, the gender schema is the lens through which individuals process incoming stimuli, including information about the self.[7] Gender schema theory proposes children learn their concepts of maleness and femaleness through interactions with others and through cultural expectations. What a child learns socially about their specific gender greatly impacts their perceptions of him or herself. These gender cues have great impact on their self-concept, as well as their own internal expectations and future goals.

A child's earliest exposure to what it means to be male or female comes from their parents. Children internalize their parents' messages regarding gender at an early age, with awareness of adult gender role differ-

---

7   Bem, 1981 & 1993

ences being found in children as young as two years old.[8] According to Raley and Bianchi,

> social psychologists and child developmental scientists suggest that a gendered self-concept emerges through a mix of social learning, biological predispositions, and gender role modeling processes that take place within the family and that result in schemas for appropriate male and female behavior and choices.[9]

In most aspects of differential treatment of boys and girls, fathers are found to discriminate more than mothers. [10,11] The gender of the parent can, at times, strongly influence the way the parent interacts, and even plays, with his or her children. Fathers engage in more physically stimulating play with their sons than with daughters, whereas mothers tend to play in a quieter way with both sexes. In childhood, fathers more than mothers, encourage "gender-appropriate" behavior and place more pressure to achieve on sons.[12]

Joseph Pleck, Ph.D, citing the work of Michale S. Kimmel, Ph.D and Michael A. Messner, states,

"The important fact of men's lives is not that they are biological males, but that they become men. Our sex may be male, but our identity as men is developed through a complex process of interaction with the culture in which we both learn the gender scripts appropriate to our culture, and attempt to modify those scripts to make them more palatable." [13,14]

---

8   Witt, 1997
9   Raley & Bianchi, 2006
10   Berk, 2000
11   Raley & Bianchi, 2006
12   Berk, 2000
13   Pleck, 1995
14   Kimmel & Messner, 1989

As children grow throughout elementary and junior high years, what happens to their psyche when they do not fit the stereotypical traits of their gender? How do children formulate a healthy concept of self when their identity does not match the information they are bombarded with by their parents, media, and the unconscious rules of society? They may ask, "Do I measure up?", "What is wrong with me?", and "Why am I different?" Some children experience this cognitive dissonance so significantly they begin to identify as transgender. Though the complex issue of transgender formation is beyond the scope of this book, my purpose herein is to examine gender development for those individuals whose gender identity is consistent with their biological sex but do not fully fit the traditional and more socially-accepted role of their gender.

A plethora of questioning and uncertainty begins in the mind of the child when this type self-examination starts. The answers to these questions can be the seeds of shame that germinate deep within the soul and eventually grow into toxic weeds of doubt and lack of identity. It can be confusing for a child to live in a world with such stark black and white definitions of gender roles and stereotypes. Their internalized message ultimately becomes, "I am defective, unworthy, and incapable", and the process of defining their gender roles begins to become confused.

SELF-REFLECTION QUESTIONS

1. *How were you introduced to your gender?*

2. *How did your parents interact with you regarding your gender?*

3. *What do you believe had the greatest impact on your gender identification?*

4. *How has your gender identity changed and developed over the years?*

5. *What are some of the earliest memories you have about your bedroom? (The décor, toys, colors, etc.?)*

6. *What are some of the earliest memories you have about the type of toys you were given to play with?*

03

ROLE OF THE FATHER

*"My father gave me the greatest gift
anyone could give another person:
He believed in me."*

— Jim Valvano

An abundance of research has been conducted about the psycho-logical effects of the presence and absence of fathers in the lives of their children. Developmental psychology textbooks will tell you the presence of a father in early development and during adolescent years is important to the overall psychological health of a child. A father's role in the life of his child is similar for both genders. However, much research has attempted to examine how the role of the father differs from sons to daughters. How does the presence or absence of a father impact each sex differently? The information presented is a mere snippet of the research available in this area. A comprehensive review of the literature from this area of research would be daunting and could fill 10 times as many pages as this book has. However, I will touch on a few highlights to spark your interest and focus on the impact of how children, especially boys, seek male attention in adolescence and adulthood.

The Role of the Father for Sons

First, let's briefly examine the role of the father in childhood, specifically in how it relates to sons. Studies have shown the strong impact of rough-and-tumble play between a father and a son, and it is believed to be a major factor in how boys learn to read the emotions of other boys and men.[15,16] Similarly, if a father displays empathy toward his son, the child can also learn that having, expressing, and sharing empathy can be a positive male characteristic.

Phillip Zimbardo, author of *The Demise of Guys*, cites that 40 percent of children in the United States are born to single mothers, and about a third of boys are raised in father-absent homes. He also reports America leads the industrialized world in fatherlessness. Zimbardo quotes David Walsh, the founder of Mind Positive Parenting, saying,

> I think that we are neglecting our boys tremendously. The result of that is that our boys aren't spending time with mentors, with elders, who can show them the path, show them the way of how it is that we're supposed to behave as healthy men. Fatherless boys may seek identity and belongingness through other unhealthy

15   Jarvis, 2010
16   Mellen, 2002

avenues such as gangs, bullying groups, and a host of addictive behaviors such as drugs, alcohol, gambling, sex, and gaming.

Consistent with previous researchers' work, Zimbardo also identified problematic behaviors positively correlated with "Father Absence"[17]. Father Absence, a term that emerged in the 60s, describes the condition of children who had never lived with both biological parents because the parents never co-habitated, or they had separated. The term Father Absence is typically not used to refer to children who experienced the death of a parent. Researchers in the 1960s were concerned with the potential impact the lack of a father had in the lives of children. Many of these issues are still examined in today's literature as well.

Father absence

Many concerns exist for the current generation of boys. It may not be that the father is absent, but the father is out of the home working long hours or multiple jobs. The child isn't afforded many opportunities to interact with his dad due to the great demands placed on him. I have had numerous boys and men of all ages sit in my office and recount stories of feeling lost and abandoned because of an absent father or a father who was physically or emotionally unavailable.

William Pollack wrote that Father Absence has been correlated with a host of ills for boys: diminished self-esteem, depression, delinquency, violence, crime, gang membership, academic failure, and difficulties with emotional commitments.[18] Edward Kruk, Ph.D. from the University of British Columbia specializes in child and family policy. He has identified a pattern of problems in children when Father Absence, Deficit,

---

17   Zimbardo, 2012
18   Pollack, 1998

and Hunger are present. Kruk reports both boys and girls who experience varying degrees of Father Absence have a diminished self-concept; compromised physical and emotional security; feelings of abandonment; bouts of self-loathing; difficulties with social adjustment; are more likely to have problems with friendships; are more truant and have poor academic performance; have higher high school dropout rates; and have higher rates of delinquency and youth crime, including violent crimes. They can also be more promiscuous and have more teen pregnancies; develop more problems with sexual health; drug and alcohol abuse; end up homeless; suffer exploitation and abuse; and have more physical health problems and mental health disorders.[19] From my own personal experience counseling men over the last 20 years, I have seen the detrimental impact of Father Absence. Often, the undesirable behaviors, like those listed above, will be what brings the patient into my office, but it is not uncommon that the underlying root of the pain is the phenomenon of Father Absence and Father Hunger. Consider the following example of how Father Absence manifested itself in the life of Kyle.

CASE EXAMPLE

Kyle, now 32 years old, remembers how his father left him, his mother, and his 6-year-old sister when he was only 4 years old. Kyle's family lived in poverty in inner city Detroit. When Kyle's father left the family, never to be heard from again, the mother, McKenna, had to get a second job waitressing at night to support her children. McKenna could not afford a babysitter, so Kyle, at the age of 4, was left in the care of his 6-year-old sister. Living in the inner city, Kyle and his sister spent many nights fearful

19   Kruk, 2012

for their safety, listening to gunshots outside their bedroom window on the street below. He grew up worrying about himself and his sister. The two often clung together, would not go anywhere without the other, and slept in the same bed well into their teen years. As a result, Kyle is now an adult who suffers with debilitating anxiety and panic attacks, struggles with anger management issues, and will go into rages when he does not feel safe.

Throughout the course of therapy, Kyle was able to identify the origin of his anxiety and panic attacks: the fear and terror he felt on a regular basis during his childhood. His anger was generated by the absence of his father, and he lives with a deep-rooted fury directed at a man he barely remembers. He is angry for being abandoned; angry his mother had to work all the time to feed them; angry his father was not around to protect him. On a deeper level, Kyle can recognize growing up without a father and living with anxiety, panic, and anger has chronically made him feel like less of a man. He admitted that living with a significant level of constant fear often leads to panic attacks and makes him feel weak. Kyle would often say, "I am supposed to be strong: a man is meant to be a protector, not bound by fear." His greatest anger towards his father comes from Kyle's own perception of his compromised masculinity. However, others are usually unaware of Kyle's level of anxiety. He will either leave the upsetting situation inconspicuously or he will explode with anger. Most people would not have the emotional depth to understand that his episodes of rage stem from fear and panic.

The Role of the Father for Daughters

The role of the father is important in the healthy development of girls as well. In her book, *Strong Fathers, Strong Daughters: The 30 Day Challenge*, pediatrician Meg Meeker describes how a father acts as a template for all male figures and roles in her life such as teachers, boyfriends, her husband, uncles, and even God himself.[20] A girl's relationship with her father is the first relationship she will ever have with a man. Often, our first experiences with a given behavior, person, or situation creates a template and ingrained perception we will use when we encounter the same or similar behaviors, persons, or situations in our future. Take a moment and think about what your template for a father is. Imagine, if the father is abusive or violent, how a girl might, from then on, perceive all men to be aggressive in a similar manner. If this were the case, what type of partner do you think she will seek out as an adult? She may develop a proclivity for aggressive men who are abusive, either verbally or physically. That being said, she may act conversely and seek to avoid the male aggression she has experienced with her abusive father. She might go to the opposite extreme, reject the template her father has set for her, and find a loving, caring man in an attempt to resolve the issue in a healthier manner than in the first scenario. There is also some risk that she could potentially just totally shut down her own emotions and struggle to cope with feelings or emotionally connect in relationships. In this possibility, she'll have learned that emotions are painful and not to be trusted, so avoidance is the best way to survive.

Father hunger and father wound

Sometimes, the problems associated with having an absent father develop into other deeper psychological pain. Since the early 1990s,

---

20   Meeker, 2016

there has been much written about the concepts of "Father Hunger" and the "Father Wound". Father Hunger, proposed by psychiatrist Jim Herzog in 1982, describes the strong desire within all children to connect with their fathers. For years, developmental and personality theorists have examined the impact that the same-sex parent has on a child's maturation. Some authors have determined the role of the father to be different for boys than for girls. [21]

It is a normal for a boy to want to connect with his father. Boys yearn for an emotional bond and connection with a dad who can teach them, validate them, and play with them. When the role of the father is not met, it is believed the child experiences a deep longing for the father, which has been called Father Hunger, as earlier described. Kyle recalls longing for his father, not only on those dark, fearful nights, but also during times he needed a man in the house to talk about things only a dad could understand and to teach him the ins and outs of boyhood.

Richard Rohr, a well-known author and lecturer, explains Father Hunger as,

> [The] need [for] him to like us, to bless us even after our mistakes, to enjoy our company, to tell us that we can succeed … If manhood itself does not like me, then I'm forever insecure about my own. His affirmation is 10 times more important than that of any other man, and of a completely different quality than the affirmation of a woman.[22]

Rohr asserts that boys need a male to give them affirmation, set limits for them, and teach them about being a man. As Rohr continued his

---

21   Witt, 1997
22   Bruno, 2013

work, he found the Father Wound to be even bigger and deeper than he had first expected in his early work.

> There is a Father Hunger in society that is unrecognized, unnamed, not seen as that. It is seen in the people who rage toward society, and in the need for authority — for someone else to tell them what to do. Underneath all of that there is a Father Wound out of which comes a tremendous Father Hunger in our society that is showing its face in so, so many ways.[23]

The trauma caused by Father Absence and Father Hunger can have a significant impact on the life and development of girls and can deeply affect their later interactions with men. Kruk reports girls also manifest an object hunger for males, and when they experience the emotional loss of their father egocentrically as a rejection of who they are, they become susceptible to exploitation by other adult men. [24]

In my own practice, I frequently hear stories from men who have been sexually exploited by someone who took advantage of their need to fill the emotional void left by an absent father. I counsel teens who actively engage in sexual activity to experience a sense of intimacy and connection with another individual, both in a heterosexual and homosexual context. A common phrase I often use when speaking to teens or working with a teen in individual therapy is, "Girls use sex to get love, and boys use love to get sex." I warn teen girls that a teenage boy's sexual advances are typically for gratification. A boy may tell a girl he loves her or has deep feelings for her if he thinks there might be a chance to be sexually gratified. A girl may offer herself sexually to a boy in the hope he will love her — she believes if she gives him sex, he will feel a deep

---

23   Rohr, 1990
24   Kruk, 2012

connection to her, claim her, and she will feel wanted and loved. To be fair, not *all* boys manipulate girls, and not *all* girls offer themselves sexually. However, I see this pattern all too often in teenagers. Yes, some of these actions are a part of teenage love and sexual exploration, but unfortunately, I see these behaviors happen more frequently when the teen is lacking a parental figure or has lacked some needed degree of nurturance from caregivers.

Fatherless women

In her article, "Fatherless Women: What Happens to the Adult Woman who was Raised Without her Father?", Gabriella Kortsch, Ph.D. writes,

> If the little girl does not have a relationship with the father, if she sees rejection or emotional coldness or withdrawal in him, or if he simply is not available at all, her sense of self will be tainted, her self-confidence warped or non-existent, her portrait of a loving relationship may be distorted or dysfunctional, and she may find herself — no matter how pretty, vivacious, lovable, funny, or intelligent — lacking in appeal.

Kortsch continues discussing how important it is for a girl to be assured of her value as a woman through this early relationship with the father. If the female has lacked the important influence of a father, she may find it difficult to relate to men, precisely because she may unconsciously seek that recognition in the eyes of a young man or even a string of young men, potentially leading her down an early path of promiscuity. [25]

There have been entire books devoted to the topic of fatherless or father-wounded girls and how it can impact their intimacy as adults. One such

---

25   Kortsch, n.d.

book is *Women and Their Fathers: The Sexual and Romantic Impact of the First Man in your Life*, written by Victoria Secunda. She writes,

> If a woman does not have a dependable nurturing father, due to his arrested development or divorce, she may believe she is essentially unlovable and seek out men who deny her needs or reject her. These women may become sexually active prematurely. They may fear intimacy. The common theme is an inability to trust, to believe that a man won't go away.

The girl comes to believe that a man won't stay present with her and will flee upon a whim. There are multiple ways a man can become arrested in the process of development. Hurting individuals produce hurting individuals. [26]

It is imperative fathers recognize the paramount importance of being involved in their children's lives. Men often make the mistake of thinking a daughter needs only her mother and leave the majority of the caregiving of girls to the mother. However, it is so important for a girl to interact with her father so that she may learn about the opposite sex. Girls who have grown up without a connection to their fathers will often complain of a void in their heart, a need to search for a connection with a male, and a desire for attention from a male counterpart. In my practice, I have seen fatherless teen girls use their sexuality to gain this attention and be in relationships with men who are abusive or give them just enough attention to string them along. Meanwhile, the young lady is giving herself sexually and doing everything she can to maintain the attention of the boy. I have seen teenage girls grow into women who repeatedly find themselves in unhealthy relationships, all for the quest of filling the void left by her father. This results in fatherless chil-

26   Secunda, 1993

dren creating more fatherless children. The impact of fatherlessness is a significant wound for children of both sexes and it manifests itself in multiple stages of life.

Rohr postulates that men struggle with how to show themselves to their children. A child can know what dad does, the role he plays in the family, how much money he earns, and the opinions he holds, but still fail to know their father on a personal level. He believes men have to be mentored by men and live in the experience with other men through relationships. [27]

What if the dad is present but doesn't pay attention to the child or demands too much of him or her? The concept of "Father Wound" is different from "Father Hunger." A Father Wound is thought to emerge when a child is denied a relationship with their father either through emotional abandonment or through violence, abuse, or neglect. When a father rejects a child by ignoring, criticizing, or refusing to acknowledge them, or responds with violence, physical rejection, or overwhelming demands, a Father Wound can develop. Many men have a deep desire to have a child, but when they do, they are often hard on them, and the child ultimately feels rejected or abandoned by the father. This can result in a Father Wound, caused by the powerful weapons of abuse, neglect, and relentless expectations.

CASE EXAMPLE

Let us consider the following example of a Father Wound. Bryce grew up with an active father, Tom, who took him to see NBA games since he was young. Tom could not wait for Bryce to grow

---

27   Rohr, 1990

past his toddler years so he could begin participating in basketball. Tom did everything he could to train his son to be tough and strong in order to be the best possible basketball player. He would often take Bryce outside and throw the basketball at him with more force than he could maneuver. Sometimes, these sessions would result in Bryce being physically hurt and emotionally shamed for not being masculine enough. Tom would call him derogatory names such as "wimp" and "sissy," and tell him he had to toughen up if "he was going to be as good at basketball as his ole' man is." This type of behavior and dialog lasted well into Bryce's high school years. However, Bryce got into trouble during his high school years for possession of marijuana. He was caught smoking with some fellow team players in the school parking lot after basketball practice. Admittedly, Bryce reported he could no longer take the pressure his father put on him, and he felt like he was a disappointment to his family. Marijuana numbed his pain caused from his Father Wound that had developed over the past decade of abuse.

When a Father Wound occurs, the child enters into a realm of toxic shame that causes him or her to begin questioning his or her own value and worth. Toxic shame, discussed in later chapters, often leads to depression. Sigmund Freud defined depression as "anger turned inward." Even though it is safe to say having a Father Wound can impact children of either gender, the majority of the research concerning Father Wounds examines how this phenomenon impacts males. Let's consider the following information.

A son may become angry and even enraged by the rejection of his father. The boy is too small and often powerless to stop the abuse or neglect.

He has two options: project and act out the rage toward others or turn it inward and attack the self. Eventually, he will have to search for ways to self-affirm through sports, academia, or some other achievement. Or, conversely, the unhealthy emotional state can lead to psychological issues such as depression, sexual aggression, and addiction, to name a few, all in an effort to self-affirm, even if it is through negative means. He may additionally resort to bullying others to externalize his pain.

Boys who experience Father Absence, Father Hunger, or a Father Wound may be more vulnerable than girls to experience gender role conflict. Without a father, the young son is more apt to be unsure about masculine ideals due to a lack of modeling and teaching. He may be at risk of feeling inferior to other boys who have masculine role models. The boy may question how he is supposed to act in social settings or may struggle with not knowing how to play sports because no one has ever taught him how to throw or catch a baseball, shoot hoops, or hurl a football through the air. A son may have other interests that have been influenced by a mother or a sister, which might make him feel self-conscious. For example, he may be more interested in the arts and creative activities, and thus, may be perceived by others as effeminate. Whatever the reason, a boy lacking the helpful influence of a male, especially a father, in his life is more prone to gender role conflict.

Within my practice, I have counseled men who, while experiencing a history of sexual abuse from important men in their lives, admit they continued to return to their abuser and may have even initiated the sexual contact, because of their Father Wound. As children, these patients wanted so desperately to be noticed, accepted, and loved by another male that they believed abuse was the only way to get these needs met. Through the abuse, they could experience the fulfillment of the vacuum they felt inside for the attention of another man, even if only for a moment.

Jonas is a prime example of this concept. His father was an angry drunk most of his life, so his local priest took over the role of the nurturing male in his life. Sadly, at some point, this alleged nurturing relationship turned sexual. For the next 22 years, Jonas would call this priest to "spend time" with him. Jonas and the priest continued their secretive sexual relationship until he was 37 years old. Jonas struggled as an adult in his heterosexual relationships and in his relationship with his daughters, and frequently changed jobs due to his problematic interactions with authority figures. Jonas finally decided to seek therapy because he could not seem to break this detrimental cycle.

In my long experience treating sexual addictions, adult men, both homosexual and heterosexual, have confessed to engaging in sexual acts with other men as a result of the Father Wound. The craving for another man's attention and affection is so deep, he begins to think the only way to experience this acceptance is to offer himself sexually. However, these encounters are *ego-dystonic*, meaning the behaviors are not congruent with the person's idealized views of the self. This act has left many heterosexual men confused about their behavior and their identity. Some men understand where the sexual desire for another man originates, while other men act out sexually and have little understanding of why they are driven to this behavior and why these acts seemingly "happen out of nowhere." Naturally, when these behaviors are ego-dystonic, they breed layers of deep shame that continue to pile up.

One explanation for the underlying dynamic that can drive heterosexual men to seek out homosexual experiences is the concept of "trauma bonds." Trauma bonds were first proposed by Patrick Carnes, Ph.D. and are described in detail in his book, *The Betrayal Bond: Breaking Free of*

Exploitive Relationships. In relation to the Father Wound, Carnes theorizes that the source of the trauma is from a history of abuse or neglect.[28]

My earlier discussion referencing the work of Pia Melody established that neglect is a form of abuse, which can be even more damaging than physically and sexually abusive acts themselves. Research by K.L. Walsh et al. has backed up this claim that chronic emotional abuse and neglect can be as devastating as physical abuse and sexual molestation.[29] Neglect is a betrayal of a child's Bill of Rights, as discussed earlier. Neglect can be a major source of shame and deep longing within the male. The male turns to potential unhealthy ways to negate the neglect. This can happen through random, anonymous sex; the development of sexual liaisons with other men in secrecy; or the act of seeking out a regular male sex partner where the meetings become a repetition of trauma.

A quick glance at the personal ads on Craigslist will give you a picture of this type of trauma being played out. The following ads were taken directly from Craigslist personals:

> *"Young, good looking straight guy seeking an older married white guy for safe fun. I have a fiancée, and am very closeted and very straight acting. I am professional, white-collar guy."*

> *"Older married looking for younger married guy."*

> *"Married, 44yrs old, 6ft. 180 lb. looking for another bi-curious, mature, married male, 45 to 60 for possibly long-term."*

---

28   Carnes, 1997
29   Walsh, 2007

As I read these, I sense the underlying trauma. I suspect these men are acting out their painful pasts that led them to seek this type of connection with another man. I can imagine the shame and secrecy surrounding them. As you can see, the behaviors birthed from trauma can take many forms, often perpetuating pain, shame, and more secrets. These traumas create a pattern for certain behaviors they may wrestle with for a lifetime.

Naturally, not every man who experiences a Father Wound will turn to another man for comfort. However, it is important to note how significant the role of a father figure is in a boy's life. The guidance and nurturance from another male can be paramount to the development of a young boy. The role of the father, or a male mentor, provides important information concerning social engagement, sex, sexuality, and intimacy.

On the other hand, there are many single parent families in today's world and are most often single mothers raising children on their own. Not every boy or girl who is raised without a father will experience emotional turmoil from the absence. Vulnerability is not always predictable, as different people are vulnerable to different things. Some boys without a father grow up to be healthy men, while others experience problems with understanding their masculinity and struggle with gender role conflict or confusion concerning sexuality. For some, their Father Wound becomes traumatic, leaving them to seek ways to cope with their emotions, whether healthy or unhealthy.

I once heard a statement that I often use in therapy, "The only difference between a rut and a grave is how long you decide to stay there." I firmly believe this. Our hurts, habits, and hang-ups only have to be temporary ruts: they do not have to become our graves. We do not have to live a lifetime of deep pain. Trauma can be dealt with and resolved.

SELF-REFLECTION QUESTIONS

1. *How did your father play and interact with you as a child?*

2. *If you have experienced Father Hunger, what are you lacking and desiring from interactions with males at this point in your life?*

3. *If you have a Father Hunger, what, if any, problematic behaviors have developed as a result?*

4. *If you have a Father Wound, what was the origin of your wound? Was it from some type of abuse or neglect? Can you define the abuse?*

5. *To what degree has your Father Hunger or Father Wound produced feelings of shame or a desire for secrecy?*

6. *How can you use your experience and pain to relate to others?*

7. *If you are a father, what template have you created for the role of the father in your child's mind?*

04

ROOTS OF GENDER CONFLICT

"Your understanding of your inner self holds the meaning of life."

— Leo Tolstoy

Throughout this book, you will read stories of men who experienced the interplay between gender role conflict, toxic shame, and complex trauma. Their experiences are a combination of ongoing traumas as a result of parental issues, being a non-traditional male, gender role conflict, social rejection, bullying, gender identity development, and the battle of self-acceptance.

The men in these stories have no desire to dishonor their parent(s), as many of them genuinely believe their parent(s) did the best they could with the information available to them. Some of their mothers were raised with sisters, with no experience of the male childhood experience or rearing boys. In some cases, the mother was trying hard to be both mother and father. In one case, the father loved the son the best way he knew how, but the boy was still raised in a home in which child labor laws were clearly violated. Other men reported their mothers felt compelled to compensate for the absence or abuse of a father. This journey is not about finding blame but about examining the process and the inner psyche of male children, adolescents, and men who struggled in their development.

These stories exam the process of development in the lives of males who "do not fit the mold." I want the words written within these pages to be a learning tool for parents, therapists, and people in pain who are struggling with gender role conflict, toxic shame, complex trauma, and self-acceptance. These struggles do not have to lead to destruction and unhealthy behaviors. Many men have triumphed over these issues, found hope, clarity, healing, and change, and have gone on to live rewarding, successful lives.

As a foundation, the book will closely recount Ben's story. Ben was raised in a strict Christian environment. His father had greatly struggled in his own developmental process with an abusive disengaged father and a mother with a disability. Ben's father had no adequate role model to look up to when it came time to be a parent himself. As a result of his father's upbringing, Ben, in turn, struggled with his own identity development through issues of Father Hunger and an overly attached mother.

The Beginning

Ben's account begins with his earliest memories of being in church at the age of four. His family attended church on a consistent basis. The music was good, and he remembers enjoying hearing the people sing and the full sound of the Hammond B-3 organ. Since service was typically long, Ben brought a red bag, sewn by his mother, to keep him entertained. In fact, he can't remember ever going to church without his red bag which contained his two favorite toys: his cars and his Barbie dolls.

His red bag was a long, rectangular pouch. Others found his bag interesting and a few older women at church would on occasion stop him to ask about the bag. They laughed and called it his "purse". At the time, Ben did not understand why they found this so amusing, though he recalls feeling a vague sense of embarrassment and misunderstanding. Feeling a sense of shame, Ben would attempt to hide behind his mother and escape the strange interaction. This was typical behavior for Ben, as he was shy and remained this way until about age 12.

During church, he would pull out a few cars, climb off the hard wooden pew, and slide down onto the carpeted floor. He slept on these pews and on this floor many times during early years. One particular Sunday, he remembers running his cars on the floor while pretending he was driving in a boundless, open field. He had plenty of room and could roll around from the pew in front of him to the back of his parents' pew and not disturb anyone.

While he drove the Matchbox car, he rolled up to the pew in front of him. The adults were standing, including the lady in a skirt in the pew in front of his. He remembers stealthily moving closer so he could look up her skirt. He had done this before, and would take a look when he could. Why he did this was a mystery to him, but he knew he must be quick and never get caught. He was a little confused by what he saw, as there were many layers — underwear, a girdle, pantyhose — so many things were covering it ... well, he didn't know what it actually was. His curiosity about girls had been growing. He knew girls were different than boys but had never seen *how*. As planned, he did not linger long. He drove his car away from the pew and scurried back to his proper spot.

Looking back on these years, Ben recalls a normal curiosity about girls and the female body. It is typically around the age of 5 for boys and girls to begin to exhibit curiosity about the differences between the sexes and understand that biological sex is permanent — at least at this age. He knew girls were different from boys, but wasn't sure how, except that girls didn't have a penis.

At some point during the church service he became bored with his cars. He remembers, at times, getting into trouble because the wheels of the cars were too loud on the wooden pew. He grabbed the red bag and pulled out his doll. Barbie was pretty and he liked to look at her, especially at her naked body, which was so different than what he knew from being male. But, he also enjoyed dressing her in fancy clothes, twisting her hair into weird designs, and making the doll into a stunning masterpiece of a woman.

Like other children, he had no understanding of gender, gender norms, or gender roles at this age. He had no idea people at church were giving him strange looks, and no idea that the old ladies were laughing at him or making fun of him for having a cloth bag full of Barbie dolls. He was content and happy, enjoying his toys. He thought to himself: wouldn't my parents have told me if there was a problem with my toys? They didn't, so it didn't occur to him to question his interest.

Ben's sister was six years older and played with Barbie dolls until the age of 10. His doll interest was piqued and developed through watching her, and he even inherited her Barbie "cast-offs" to begin his own collection.

Ben's fascination and collection of toy cars was a different story. His mother, strongly governed by routine, always followed a specific weekly schedule. She grocery shopped on Monday afternoons, so Ben was left in the care of his loving grandmother. His mother brought a new car home to him every Monday. He would wait with great anticipation to see what it would be: a new ambulance? Maybe a race car? A Rolls Royce, perhaps?

He doesn't recall purchasing dolls but remembers going through store aisles looking for new outfits. He would also attempt to make clothes out of extra material his mother had used on her past sewing projects. She was a proficient seamstress and was amused at his attempt to sew Barbie doll clothes. At times, she would make clothes he requested for the dolls. The maternal involvement reinforced his belief that Barbie dolls were an acceptable toy for boys and this type of play was consistent with other boys' activities and interests. Ben had a strong connection to his dolls; they were of great value to him and not something he played with casually and tossed aside when done.

As a clinical psychologist, I believe it is healthy for children to play with cross-gender toys. It is beneficial for a boy to learn how to hold a baby doll, and for a girl to learn to protect herself playing with a G.I. Joe. Children often learn about the gender roles and potentially the emotions of the opposite gender through the action of play and the use of fantasy and creativity.

This was a peaceful time in Ben's life, as the demands of the world had not yet started. He didn't have friends yet since his family lived outside of the city limits and there were few opportunities for play-dates and social interaction. He mostly played independently at home. He was strongly attached to his mother and would follow her from room to room, learning many domestic skills, such as cooking, and was able to do laundry by age 10.

Unfortunately, other than at the dinner table, Ben has little recollection of his father's presence at home. His father was a quiet, yet ambitious man who was busy building independent wealth, as he had come from meager means. During Ben's developmental years, his father was often absent from the home because he was working his job, a side job, or seeing to an array of small businesses he had acquired. Financially, his ambition provided well for Ben's family, but his mother was left with the primary care and rearing of the children.

His father did not interact with him much. Ben was told that as a baby, he didn't like when his father held him and would cry incessantly when he picked him up. Though his father was not highly interactive or consistently engaged with Ben, he never seemed bothered by Ben's behavior or his choice in toys, nor was he ever abusive or unkind.

At a young age, however, Ben started to feel the impact of Father Absence. He knew his father was distant and not actively involved in his life. As he approached adolescence, the lack of a father's presence in his life impacted him on a deeper, more confusing level. He lacked a male role model and failed to experience the "rough and tumble" kinetic play, focus on sports, and the male development that typically occurs from such gender-specific interaction. The heavy involvement and guidance of his mother also made a mark on his psyche by feminizing his masculinity.

As previously addressed in Chapter 3, though biological sex is determined at conception, gender identity is developed through a complex process of interaction with parents, siblings, friends, and the culture in which we develop. We assimilate gender scripts and alter these scripts to fit our specific circumstances.

Ben's gender script had started to alter. At a young age, he had limited exposure to other boys and had strongly attached to the two individuals most present in his world: his mother and sister. His choice of toys came from a mix of his sister's influence and toys that had been purchased for him. His perceptions of the world were taking shape; however, he had no idea that what he was experiencing was a skewed roadmap for male maturation.

During the course of therapy, Ben often voiced that he wished his parents had tried to curtail his strong attachment to the dolls. He believes his parents more than likely assumed he would grow out of this stage and develop different interests; however, he did not. As an adult, Ben sees the intense attachment to the dolls as a critical component to the beginnings of his struggle with gender role confusion.

Though thankful for a hard-working father, what was the impact of Father Absence on his life? With limited exposure to a male role model who could help him understand the differences and nuances of two different genders, Ben was not provided with a masculine model to mimic. Consequently, his actions and behaviors became more feminized due to his attachment to the females in his life as he continued to develop. Additionally, the continual communication and interaction between his mother and sister was influencing the manner in which he learned to communicate through mannerisms and speech prosody. A child's world can be small while the influences in it can be great.

As seen in the following clinical example of John, a recent patient of mine, sometimes the slightest event can become a root for a thought or a feeling that continues to grow. During therapy, John disclosed what he believed was the root of his gender role conflict and confusion. John viewed himself as a sensitive and emotional child. Though he had a loving mother, he describes his father as a bully during his early years. Feeling much of his strong attachment to his mother was caused by fear of his father, he spent a good portion of his formative years emulating his mother. John distinctively remembers the day an adult said to him, "You would have made a great girl." He identifies this statement, from a random person, as the root of his gender confusion. John recalls this statement continually ruminated in his mind over the next several years: it was the beginning of his self-doubt and questioning. He wondered if the lady was right: "would I have made a good girl?" This led John to the following internal questions of: "Was there a mistake?" and "Should I have been born a girl?" We will discuss John more in future chapters, as this root grew into a vine, intertwining itself throughout John's inner mind and identity.

While conducting research, I considered if books written for parents raising toddlers addressed the topic of gender. Starting with the ubiquitous best-seller, *What to Expect When You're Expecting*, I could find little, if any, discussion of gender development and the role of the expectant parent. I examined several books focused primarily upon parents raising toddlers. Again, a cursory review revealed little to no mention of the subject matter. While the concept of gender is a growing topic in today's culture, it appears woefully absent from books and sources of media that teach parents about child development. Child rearing information, from the point of conception through adolescence, needs to include information about how overt and covert actions, as well as conscious and unconscious behaviors, will guide gender formation. I am a strong proponent of pregnancy books, parenting and developmental literature including segments about gender development, and how to foster proper gender identification for the intended outcome.

Children receive gender direction from both conscious and unconscious messages in their environment. Therefore, it is imperative that parents, day care workers, and all child caregivers who interact with children understand how a child's gender develops. A variety of influences can become the roots of feelings, behaviors, and ideas in the life of a child.

There are numerous environmental factors that can play a role, as well. The encouragement of cross-gender activities and play, Father Absence, strong presence of an overly involved opposite-sexed parent, the influence of opposite-sexed siblings during formative years, and overall communication with a child — these are all examples of ways gender identification is imprinted on the psyche of the young mind and can become the roots of gender role conflict.

SELF-REFLECTION QUESTIONS

1. *What were your favorite toys as a child?*

2. *Did you play with cross-gendered toys, and, if so, what was your favorite?*

3. *Do you see any roots of gender role conflict in the early stages of your development?*

4. *How did you learn about the physical differences between the genders?*

5. *What role did your parents play in your gender development?*

05

THE TRINITY OF DESTRUCTION: ABUSE, TRAUMA, AND SHAME

"The truth is that it hurts because it is real.
It hurts because it mattered.
And that's an important thing
to acknowledge to yourself."

— John Green

You cannot read trauma literature today without hearing about various types and definitions of trauma. Studies have examined the origins, durations, frequencies, and the effects of various traumas on individuals and their associated mental, social, and physical development.

Type I and II Trauma

Lenore Terr, Ph.D. proposes two distinct types of trauma.[30] Type I trauma is an isolated, single event that feels like it happens in slow motion. It leaves the victim with the ability to recall minute details and descriptions of the event. Many people who experience natural disasters and car accidents report Type I trauma. Type II trauma is an ongoing traumatic situation. Continual sexual or physical abuse is an example of Type II trauma. Naturally, the first time this type occurs, it takes the victim by surprise, often resulting in profound shock. Upon subsequent traumatic occurrences, the child is forced to develop mental strategies to process the trauma. The victim may construct a mental wall of denial, push the memory deep into the mind through repression, or learn to self-hypnotize and disassociate while the abuse occurs. Terr theorizes that both Type I and Type II traumas can be so emotionally painful that the memories of the event can be repressed within the individual's mind and not emerge until much later in life.

Trauma comes from many different sources and often manifests itself through some form of abuse. Abuse is a broad word used by many people in many different contexts. What is an actual definition of abuse? Though it varies according to author and clinician, Pia Melody and Claudia Black define abuse as "any action, or inaction, taken by a caregiver that is less than nurturing or experienced as shaming."

I know this definition seems wide sweeping. Its broadness initially struck me; however, as I pondered this, I slowly came to a point of agreement. When a caregiver fails to provide something to a child, whether it is emotional or physical, it has a great effect on the child's development. Many people see neglect as differing from abuse, but I propose it is

---

30   Terr, 1994

another form of abuse. Neglect can be as damaging to the development of a child as overt abuse. When children experience events that are less than nurturing, they tend to ascribe meaning to the event or themselves.

Big-T trauma and Small-t trauma

Let us examine some statements that fall under the category of abusive. Some appear innocuous upon first glance while others are blatantly abusive and clearly identified. However, both can have harmful consequences to a child's development. Physical abuse is the most readily identified. Statements such as, "my dad used to tie us to a tree outside, put a black garbage bag over our heads, and hit us with a two-by-four", clearly fall under the definition of physical abuse. Francine Shapiro, PhD. is the developer of EMDR (Eye Movement Desensitization and Reprocessing), an effective form of psychotherapy for resolving the symptoms of traumatic life experiences. At one point in the development of her technique, she proposed the idea that trauma could be categorized according to severity. Examples such as the acute physical abuse exemplified above are categorized as "Big-T trauma". Sexually overt trauma is also categorized as a Big-T trauma. Statements of sexual abuse, such as, "my mother was lonely and used to have me lie and caress her breasts", and/or rape experiences would both qualify as Big-T trauma. This type of trauma will often lead to Post-Traumatic Stress Disorder (PTSD). Shapiro defines "Small-t trauma" as abuse that might not be readily identifiable by others but can be overwhelming to the individual experiencing the trauma. It may consist of the abandonment or the humiliation of a child and can be much more difficult to identify as abusive in nature. These types of abusive situations are, for example, paternal statements such as "we really only wanted two kids" or "it's a good thing your sister is smart enough to take over the family business". It is the Small-t traumas that are often overlooked, cast off, and not recognized as abuse by either the victims themselves or by the general public. In academic literature, you will find Small-t traumas can also be referred to as "complex trauma". The trauma has occurred over a period of time, adding layer upon layer, and has become interwoven in the psyche of the person, leading to a complex internal trauma experience. The concept of complex trauma will be explored more in Chapter 10. Since the development of the concept of Big-T trauma and Small-t trauma, Shapiro has moved away from making a clear distinction between the two and has now referred to them as "Adverse Life Events", using the term as an umbrella for all traumas. This moves the thought of trauma away from the ability to classify one as worse than the other, and helps people understand all Adverse Life Events have the rudiments of a trauma experience.

The use of Big-T and Small-t trauma sub-classifications within this book is to help you conceptualize the concept of trauma in a more intricate manner. With the knowledge that trauma can be subtle at times, it is important individuals and clinicians have a mental framework to understand ALL traumas. Whether of the Big-T or Small-t classification, they can still be equally catastrophic to the person living through the experience. Every individual is born unique and has their own pre-dispositions: what is traumatic for one may not be so for another. However, one individual cannot make judgments about another person's experience of trauma and whether, indeed, it was truly traumatic to the victim.

The next portion of this chapter examines Adverse Life Events, but will continue to classify them as Big-T traumas and Small-t traumas to help you understand the construct. An example of Small-t abuse is intellectual abuse. Think of the psychological damage to a child when he or she hears a parent say, "You're such a disappointment. Where did I go wrong?" or "They just don't grow them very smart here in Pennsylvania". Statements such as these attack the child's self-esteem and their ideas of self-efficacy and potency. The child may begin to internalize the idea that they are unintelligent and inferior to other children. These statements then become a filter through which other statements, whether hurtful or benign, may be translated into an increasingly harmful internal message. Referring back to the material in Chapter 1, in which we examined how vital it is for children to have a strong sense of self-worth and feel equal to others, we can now understand how hurtful messages made by the adults closest to those children allow shame to set in and become toxic.

CASE EXAMPLE

Early in my career, Janice brought her 9-year-old son, Calvin, to my office for therapy. Calvin was the youngest of five other siblings. During the first session, Janice clearly stated, "Calvin is probably my child that is not so bright; he has some siblings who are rather smart and do well academically." I quickly took note that Janice was willing to directly say this while in Calvin's presence. Initially, Calvin did not show any mental or personal deficits other than some minor behavioral issues. As the weeks progressed, I did not find any problems with Calvin's intellectual abilities or aptitude. I did notice, however, his immature behavior gained him personal attention from Janice (though not positive in nature), which he would rarely find otherwise within the large family. As I continued to occasionally meet with her, she would continue to make her statement about Calvin not being "one of her bright children". Not believing this was an accurate assessment of Calvin, I administered the Wechsler Intelligent Assessment for Children. As I suspected, Calvin scored in the upper 130s, placing him in the Superior Range of Intellectual Functioning. I reported the results to

Janice and watched the shock attack her body, like a frigid wind. Initially, she argued the accuracy of the results. I informed her of my belief that Calvin's behavioral issues stemmed from her constant statements about his inferior intelligence. Over the course of therapy, I was able to help Janice adjust the way she spoke to and about Calvin. As a result, he progressed out of his immature behavior, and he was able to find his place within the rest of her intelligent family clan.

Emotional abuse

Emotional abuse can come in many forms. Think about the parent who screams, "I should have aborted all you kids" or the father who announces in anger, "you were a waste of sperm." These sound extreme, as if even from a movie script, but unfortunately, these are both phrases I have heard from my clients as they have processed their own stories of abuse and trauma. Alternatively, parents will make offhanded comments when tired or frustrated that are harmful to a child. This is not done with ill intentions but more frequently are a projection or a reaction to a current situation or emotional state. How does a child interpret his or her worth when they hear a parent say, "You exhaust me?"

CASE EXAMPLE

Let us consider Bart, an emotional 6-year-old being raised primarily by his grandparents. His biological parents abused drugs and alcohol, disappearing for extended periods of time to an unknown location. Bart was frequently left with his grandparents while his parents were off on their next escapade. Naturally, the confusing nature of his parental relationship only made Bart more emotional. When Bart would cry, the grandfather would call him "a girl" or say, "Where is my boy? He's turned into a little girl. You should have been born a girl." This abusive taunting only continued to upset the child, contributing further to the emotional lability he displayed. Where was Grandpa's empathy? Could he not see this child was hurting and confused? Emotional abuse often creates a sense of powerlessness within the child, which causes them to believe they lack the strength or potency to live in the world effectively.

Conversely, what is the effect on the child who is falsely empowered? We have all met these children who are often referred to as "a brat" or even "a spoiled rotten brat". The term *affluenza* first started appearing in the 1950s and described a person's quest to gain status and worth through material possessions. In our culture, we frequently refer to this phenomenon as "keeping up with the Joneses". Ultimately, though, this quest leads to debt acquisition and an overall sense of emptiness and unhappiness. It is important to note the term "affluenza" is not a psychological disorder, but simply a word used to describe a problematic mindset related to wealth. Should you be interested in learning more about this mindset, Adrian Furnham, Ph.D. in a 2014 article titled "Affluenza: The psychology of wealth", published by Psychology Today, describes the unhappiness and psychic void this particular mindset can leave behind.

In modern-day culture, the term has been popularized as a result of the infamous media frenzy over the criminal defendant Ethan Couch, to whom the media referred as "The Affluenza Teen". Mr. Couch killed four people when driving while intoxicated. The defense hired psychologist G. Dick Miller to provide expert testimony. He proclaimed Ethan

Couch was a victim of affluenza. The defendant was eventually charged with four counts of intoxicated manslaughter while driving under the influence, sentenced to 10 years of probation and intensive therapy with the hope of rehabilitation. This young man is a prime example of the consequences of abusing through false-empowerment. The term "affluenza" is also applied to those who do not understand the consequences of their actions due to financial privilege. As a therapist, I question, "Did his affluence truly prohibit his moral development?" Or rather, "Were the parents of this teen neglectful in setting limits, boundaries, and fostering appropriate moral development?" In my clinical opinion, their indulgence of this teen was a serious, yet subtle, form of neglect. As you can see from our case analysis of The Affluenza Teen, neglect, even in the form of parental inaction, can be just as damaging as covert abuse.

Intergenerational shame

Intergenerational Shame is another form of abuse that may not be at the forefront of the mind of a clinician and does not appear often in the literature. This Adverse Life Event can be considered Small-t abuse but can have a significant impact on the recipient. Intergenerational Shame is a term with which most people, outside the field of psychology, have little experience. This is shame passed on from generation to generation through the process of keeping family secrets. It can be related to any type of family secret: from men in the family who have had affairs and strayed from their marriages to the family fortune that originated from criminal activity. Based on this passed-down information, the recipient may make interpretations about their worth and value as a person, or as a member of such a family. How do these family secrets affect a person's sense of worth or identity? The message translated is the belief that one's bloodline itself is shameful and should not be shared. Researchers have particularly examined the way in which family violence influences intergenerational shame.[31,32] Let's consider the toll of intergenerational shame with the example below.

What is the process of abuse that occurs when you watch another person be abused? Take the young daughter whose father sneaks into her room at night to inappropriately touch her sister. What message is sent to the daughter who is not sexually abused? She is left thinking that there is something wrong with her because her sister is "favored" by her father. Or, conversely, she is left with guilt and shame for knowing what was happening to her sister but not defending her. What is the impact of a survivor's guilt and shame in situations such as these, and what impact does this have on a child's self-esteem? I have seen all sorts of ramifications manifest from auxiliary types of abuse that leave behind a heavy burden of guilt and shame for the individual to carry.

Enmeshment

Sometimes abuse comes in the form of smothering and enmeshment. Boundaries are blurred and the child is forced to take care of the emotional wellbeing of the adult(s) in their life. A child is not equipped, cognitively or emotionally, to take on these types of responsibilities. How can a child possibly understand the complex emotional needs of an adult, especially those of a parent? These types of situations become overwhelming for the child and can stress them and lead to more feelings of shame and guilt.

31   Dutton, van Ginkel, & Starzomski, 1995
32   Ford, 2001

CASE EXAMPLE

Samantha's unfortunate situation is a prime example of damage caused from blurred parental boundaries. Samantha is a 14-year-old girl who lives with both of her biological parents and three younger siblings. Samantha is aware that there are problems between her parents, Larry and Leslie, as she often hears them arguing at night. She knows Dad's occasional drinking binges on Friday nights are a problem at times, and often lead to her parents fighting. Samantha knows her mother, Leslie, is unhappy because she and her mom will sometimes sit on the porch and talk. Leslie often confides in Samantha that she doesn't think she loves Larry anymore and that she finds him draining, personally, emotionally, and sexually. Leslie has also recently begun an affair with Joe, Samantha's younger brother's Boy Scout leader. Leslie and her children have been meeting Joe at the mall during the days to have lunch with him and often go to the movies. Samantha is left sitting close to the front of the theater, watching her three younger siblings, while Leslie and Joe sit in the back, where there is physical privacy. Leslie has made it clear that Samantha can never mention this and that Larry, especially, can never find out. Unfortunately, Samantha becomes depressed as a result of this ongoing burden and finds herself in a counseling office where she is finally able to unload the family secret and admit she has begun feeling suicidal. The pain of her mother's lack of boundaries and the responsibility of keeping this huge secret from her father is, understandably, more than a 14-year-old child can bear.

Neglect

It is also important to consider how neglect impacts the life of a child. What message does neglect give a child about his or her own sense of worth? If a child's basic needs of food, clothing, and shelter are not met, the child might reasonably interpret this neglect to mean that they are inferior to others. In their mind, if they were important, their physical needs would not be neglected. In the same way, the emotional needs of the child must be nurtured. Emotional neglect is another form of abuse; it is abuse by inaction, one of omission rather than commission, but nonetheless traumatic.

Ben

Ben's father's lack of attention and emotional nurturance and emotional neglect was detrimental to the development of his self-esteem and self-concept. He questioned his personal value; questioned his father's love; and felt inferior and unworthy. At times, the neglect resulted in self-blame, and Ben asked himself, "Why does he not like me? What could I have done to cause his distance?" As a young child, the erroneous conclusion he drew was that he must be inherently flawed in some way and did not deserve love and attention. Neglect can be as damaging to a child's psyche and development as more active forms of abuse are.

This is only a cursory overview of the types of abuse that can occur. Whatever the origin of abuse, the shame engendered from it cannot be ignored. All types of abuse are harmful. When behavior is less than nurturing, it is emotionally noticed and interpreted by the child. The experience and interpretation is often negative and can cause the child to question their sense of human worth. This becomes the root of shame that grows while the abuse is occurring and typically continues to grow long after the abuse has ceased.

SELF-REFLECTION QUESTIONS

1. *If you have experienced a trauma in your life, can you identify it as a Type I or Type II trauma, as discussed in the opening paragraphs of this chapter?*

2. *Can you identify any Big-T Traumas in your life, as defined by F. Shapiro?*

3. *Can you identify any Small-t Traumas in your life, as defined by F. Shapiro?*

4. *What is your internal reaction to the definition of abuse being anything less than nurturing?*

5. *What is your own definition of abuse?*

6. *Can you identify the types of abuse you may have experienced (physical, sexual, emotional, intellectual, neglect)?*

7. *What types of abuse have you experienced that you have never thought of as abuse?*

THE DEEPENING
OF THE CONFLICT

06

*"Without self-knowledge, without understanding
the working and functions of his machine,
man cannot be free, he cannot govern himself
and he will always remain a slave."*

— G. J. Gurdjieff

I'd like to make a more in-depth examination of Ben's early development, as previously introduced in Chapter 4. The foundation of the trauma had been laid: the Father Absence and enmeshment with his mother was in full swing by mid-elementary school. Social rejection, bullying, and self-loathing would eventually follow in middle childhood years and would build their structure upon this troubled foundation.

Daytime Soap Operas

As a young child, there was a great deal of structure in Ben's life. He knew his mother's weekly routine and followed it according to plan. Each day had an agenda laden with specific tasks to be accomplished. Among the established routines was the daily viewings of soap operas, especially *The Young and the Restless*. Still as an adult, he can tell you about characters on the show from 40 years ago when he and his mother would sit together, engrossed in the drama.

The *Young and the Restless* had many beautiful characters, and the drama was unlike anything Ben had yet experienced in real life. Back in the early 1970s, the show was centered on four sisters and their relationships with various men. Ben specifically remembers two main characters: Chris Brooks Foster and Dr. Snapper Foster. The two characters married on the show in 1974, when Ben was 5 years old. Chris was beautiful with light brown hair and tan skin. But Ben was also drawn to Snapper, although he wasn't sure why, remembering the character's brown curly hair and his masculine physique. At this young age, he did not find it confusing to feel some sense of attraction to both characters. Though he didn't understand the concept of attraction or how such instincts worked, he knew when either of them appeared on the screen he felt a sense of excitement. Their relationship was filled with turmoil and tragedy, like any other soap opera romance, and Ben was enthralled by their chemistry and struggles.

Naturally, the scenes in these shows were sexually charged. Snapper was a young, powerful doctor who had sexual relations with many women, even while engaged to his beautiful fiancée, Chris. Though he didn't fully understand what was happening on screen, Ben began to build an engrained perception that men and women seemed to function in pairs. Dr. Snapper would have his hairy chest exposed, lying in bed with a woman, while she had the sheet tightly tucked under her armpits, covering her breasts. At this point in childhood, he did not question what it meant when he enjoyed seeing both of their bodies.

In retrospect, Ben believes he was drawn to Dr. Snapper as a result of searching for a male role model — a person from whom he could subconsciously learn the rules of manhood. Snapper was a strong, powerful, good-looking doctor. Was this a man Ben should emulate? The doctor's character embodied the male ideal. He was overtly masculinized, blatantly sexual, and extremely cunning in his deception of women.

Kindergarten

When it was time for Ben to enter school, he was filled with anxiety over the thought of leaving his mother's side. Surprisingly, he recalls his concerns were for her wellbeing rather than his own forthcoming independence. Concerned about her impending loneliness, Ben would bring her his stuffed animals to keep her company while he was away.

Because of the deep enmeshment now forged between the two, his mother arranged for a close friend to take him to school on the first day of kindergarten. His mother was concerned that if she took him, he would not leave her side and would refuse to go into the classroom.

Being delivered to the elementary school by his mother's friend, he surprisingly did not cry nor fight the unfamiliar environment. He entered the classroom and sat quietly. Ben had not been exposed to many other children except briefly at church. Some of the classroom boys were fighting and throwing balls. They appeared to be playing roughly, and he did not care for the "rough and tumble" actions of this group. The girls in the room seemed much calmer, choosing to color or talk. This was Ben's first social and gender dilemma. What was he to do? With whom should he interact?

Eventually, he adjusted and became acquainted with some kindergarten classmates. It was at this time he began to have moments of self-awareness: he did not care for the boys and the sorts of activities that held their interest, the wrestling and throwing balls at one another, for example. Through his observations, he began to draw conclusions about gender interaction. He perceived boys were often mean to one another and did not frequently interact with girls. Aware of his feelings of discomfort with the boys, though also unconvinced that he fit in with the girls, he recalls feeling unwelcome in either group. He didn't like many of the girls' activities, such as playing "house" and caring for baby dolls, though he did enjoy talking and laughing with them. This was the stage in which children observe social interaction in others. The mind of a child is very observant, taking cues from the environment and deciding how to interact with the world based on those cues. A boy can learn that it may be detrimental to play with more stereotypical feminine toys in the presence of other boys, lest they risk social rejection. To make matters more difficult, children can be bold and blatant in voicing their observations about the world around.

The kindergarten teacher, concerned about Ben's behavior and adjustment, initiated a conference with his mother. With great curiosity, his mother arrived at the appointment to find the teacher expressing her opinion that Ben might be "gay" and asking if his mother had ever considered the possibility. Ben's astonished mother denied any merit to the teacher's concerns. Of course, the teacher's actions took place several decades ago when society was less accepting of various sexual orientations and lifestyles. In the past, deviations from heterosexuality were viewed as mental conditions; at the time, the teacher felt it necessary to intervene for Ben's own good.

Eventually, Ben befriended two boys, Eric and Timmy. The three of them had something in common: they all loved Matchbox and Hot Wheels cars and would play with them at school or any opportunity they were together. Eventually, they had play dates outside of school and they would play cars together for hours. Ben was happy to finally have made two male friends who did not seem to be rough like the other boys in his class. As time went on, Ben and Eric became especially close and the friendship lasted for years.

Summer

Summer returned after the kindergarten school year ended. Ben was back to playing by himself at home, unless he had a play date scheduled with Eric or Timmy. This change was welcomed, for at least he didn't feel out of place when he was alone; he could be *himself*. He could play with whatever he wanted, pretend to be whomever he wanted, and not be ashamed about choosing his Barbie dolls or kitchen set over more masculine toys. He enjoyed this freedom of solitary activity. Ben also played Cowboys and Indians outside, running around with a shiny, silver Lone Ranger handgun. He often used the neighbor's horse, Taffy, as part of his fantasy. Looking back, Ben recalls his play was a combination of both genders' stereotypical behavior. However, at the time, he was exploring his world through a child's work of play. His summer was uneventful, with one notable exception.

Ben was particularly impacted by his mother's odd decision to suddenly burn her wedding dress. She declared it was getting old and crumbly and falling apart after 20 years of storage. He remembers everyone on

TV making such a big deal about the beautiful Cinderella-type dresses, so he knew the dress must be important.

As his mother pulled it from the box, he noticed it was petite. She had only weighed 89 pounds on her wedding day when she was 19 years old. Noticing its size, Ben asked to try it on, and she agreed, helping him slip into the piles of white netting and silky material over his small frame. It nearly fit. He remembers the feel of the dress in his hands and on his skin, the heavy weight of the material pulling down on his shoulders, and even the crunchy sound of the netting as it settled around his feet. His mother went about her chores, agreeing to burn the dress later. He played in the dress, giggling out with silliness and fun. Eventually it was time for him to remove the dress.

Together, he and his mother walked up the green painted basement stairs and out into the yard, about 30 feet from where the burning barrel was located. He watched in amazement as she dumped the white dress into the black ashes of the barrel. She lit a match and, within seconds, the dress started disintegrating. It burned quickly, as the netting had become brittle over the years, flaring up immediately into a cascade of flames. He had the oddest feeling as he watched it burn. Something did not seem right about this, yet his mother didn't seem bothered by it at all. Following her lead, he also showed no emotions, remaining obser-vant. When they were finished, the two went back into the house and carried on with the day, as if it were any other.

As a child, and even into his adult years, he struggled with making sense of this strange event. He considered why one would burn their wedding dress, especially in front of their children. He wondered if there were underlying messages about marriage implied from the act. Was marriage a nuisance, and was his mother, in particular, unhappy in her marriage? As an adult he eventually questioned his mother's willingness to allow him to wear the dress. Upon conversations with her, he understood she was allowing him to have fun and she truly burned the dress simply because it was falling apart. Had he not been experiencing the underpinnings of gender role conflict, wearing the dress would have had no impact. However, he believed this summer event likely contributed to his developing confused state.

First Grade

When school resumed, Ben transferred to a new school even further from his house and now rode the bus with kids of all ages and sizes. He was frightened of the older kids. Though the younger kids typically sat up front and the older kids tended to sit in back, he, being picked up nearly last, often was forced to sit in the back of the bus with the older children.

Some of these older children engaged in what we would now call "bullying", as they ascertained he was more effeminate than many of his peers. He recalls them taking his hat, tossing it around and calling him cruel names. His older sister rode the bus, and often defended him when the older kids' torments grew excessively rough.

One particular day after school, he and two of his close friends, Jeannie and Suzie, chose to sit in the back of the bus, as the elementary students were released first from classes and finally had freedom of choice for sitting options. One of his friends started talking about "private parts." Jeannie dared Suzie and Ben to show each other "their parts". He was shocked that they wanted to see his penis. Eventually, he and Suzie agreed to unbutton their pants, and he finally saw a female's body. It was underwhelming to him, and he proceeded to show his appendage. There was much giggling before it was over.

Ben later felt a sense of guilt, feeling they might have done something inappropriate. But, being so young and uncomprehending, he decided the interaction was harmless. He now knows his interest in the female body at the time was age-appropriate, and curiosity was to be expected at that young age.

Jeannie went home and told her aunt about the incident. The aunt promptly called Ben's mother, who remained calm when later discussing the issue with him. She asked what had happened, and gently said it was important to keep that area of his body to himself. He understood and thought the situation was over but was mistaken.

Jeannie's aunt personally confronted him at church the next Sunday, pulling him aside to shame him, privately, for what had occurred. His young mind interpreted this to mean, "Wanting to see a *female body* must be a bad thing," and surmised he was not supposed to like this part of a girl. He remembers wanting someone to discuss this with him, to clarify what exactly these female body parts were and to explain the secrecy involved. He was in need of a simple explanation about the difference between boys and girls.

As you can see from Ben's experience, in addition to what I have experienced as a therapist, I believe it is a good idea for parents and/or guardians to have a preliminary discussion with their child around the ages of 4 to 6 about the biological sex differences between boys and girls. This may help to add clarity to any confusion and natural curiosity likely occurring. Also, it is an opportunity to start setting appropriate boundaries regarding potential physical exploration with other kids. Furthermore, the greatest benefit of these discussions is that parents will be setting a solid foundation for further discussion, as more questions eventually emerge about sexuality as the child grows. Parents are the best source of information for the child about such sensitive matters. Be certain: children have questions, and they will seek answers where they can find them. If a parent imparts the information they are seeking, they can appropriately encase it within a moral structure that is congruent with their family's belief system or world view and better prepare the child for adulthood.

Revelation

Macy was a few years older than Ben — she was nearly 9 years old. They would often meet at the park and ride bikes around the neighborhood. Though fun to play with, Macy was preoccupied with the male anatomy. He recalls, numerous times, her asking him to show his "private parts". At times he would oblige, and it seemed to make her happy when he would let her see it and touch it. Why was it acceptable for girls to see his private body part, but it was shameful for him to want to see theirs? He has no memory of her ever showing off her anatomy or letting him touch her similarly. He specifically recalls one day lying in the grass on the hillside of the park and her asking to touch him. She explained if she touched it for long enough, white stuff would come out. Having not yet reached puberty himself, he did not understand this, and told her "no", zipping up his pants. It wasn't until much later in life that he recognized the level of inappropriate sexual information this girl had for someone her age. Was she being abused by someone? Was she exposed to pornography that depicted such images? Where did she learn this? Though I believe it is important for parents to explain the anatomical differences of boys and girls while they are young, in my professional and personal opinion, the details of sexual functions are best reserved for children in their pubescent years.

The first explanation of sexual interaction came from another classmate during a bus ride home from first grade. A high school girl spontaneously decided to tell Ben, rather graphically, about the events that transpire during intercourse. He supposes she thought this would be funny. Though he doesn't remember her exact terminology, he walked away with the mechanics understood quite well. His penis was designed for a female's private parts, and eventually would place a baby inside a girl. He now understood this was how he was made. Did he believe what this high school girl told him? It seemed convincing, but he had never heard of anything so preposterous.

He trusted his mother and knew she would know the truth. After the encounter, he quickly scurried to the kitchen where she was peeling potatoes for dinner. "Mom", he said with a strong voice of curiosity, "this high school girl on the bus, Julianne Avery, told me how babies are made. She told me a boy puts his *thing* in the girl's *that* and leaves it there for a while and it eventually makes a baby. Is that true?" His mother stood there for a moment, gaping with the paring knife in one hand and a potato in the other. She dropped the potato into the sink and gripped the kitchen sink tightly. All she replied was, "Yes, Ben." Years later, his mother shared with him that she had to hold onto the sink because her blood went rushing out of her head and she nearly passed out for a moment.

As he pondered what he had learned, it began to make sense in his young mind. The aunt shamed him because he was too young to have children; he was still a child himself, how could he have a child? He also remembers thinking, "I get it now, I know what Chris and Snapper were doing now on the *Young and the Restless*: they were making a baby". He also recalled being grateful he enjoyed girls more than boys because he wanted children in the future and would have a better chance of this by spending time with girls instead of boys who only play with other boys. He erroneously assumed it was time to get a girlfriend.

His mission for the next school day was to find her. And he did, in the form of Beth, a girl in first grade who was beautiful, with long golden blonde hair like Rapunzel. She agreed to be his girlfriend through most of first grade.

Naturally, this was his first experience with having a girlfriend, and it provided him with a social focal point so he did not feel so out of place. At this point, he started to understand a little bit about the roles of males and females. Because he now had a girlfriend, he felt he must, at his core, be similar to most other boys.

SELF-REFLECTION QUESTIONS

1. *What television stars or characters held your attention early in life?*

2. *What did the role of that person communicate to you?*

3. *What are your memories of entering school?*

4. *Do you remember any instances of showing your body to other curious children in exchange that they do the same?*

5. *At what age was your first sexual experience?*

6. *At what age did someone discuss biological differences with you? What role did they play in your life?*

7. *When was your first "boyfriend/girlfriend" experience?*

07

SHAME

> *"Shame is the most powerful, master emotion.*
> *It's the fear that we're not good enough."*
>
> — Brene Brown

Entire books have been written about shame. From a Biblical viewpoint, shame is possibly the first emotion experienced by man, as described in Genesis Chapter 2. Adam and Eve recognized their nakedness, felt ashamed of being exposed, and ran to hide. Feelings of guilt and shame are a natural response to wrongdoing.

Psychologists have examined the emotion of "shame" extensively. It has been studied on a biological level: examining which brain structures are activated; on a physiological level: examining chemical reactions and responses; and on a cognitive level: attempting to identify the mental thoughts and components that serve as the origins of the emotion. There are many theories and postulates about the concept of shame. The short overview contained in this book is not a comprehensive study but offers a brief synopsis.

Physiological Components of Shame

Shame is multi-dimensional, originating from many physiological levels. Understanding these complex interactive systems is challenging to the layperson; however, I will try to give a cursory view of some of the physiology involved in shame.

The *autonomic nervous system* is actually made up of two systems; the sympathetic nervous system, which activates our bodies to fight, flight, or freeze; and the parasympathetic nervous system, which handles more unconscious and automatic responses. Together, the sympathetic and parasympathetic systems are believed to be able to cause two anxious states: hypervigilance, when our nervous system can become stuck in overstimulation; or conversely, dissociative states, when our nervous system becomes stuck in a state of inaction.

The *central nervous system*, consisting of the brain and spinal cord, transmits messages throughout the body. The midbrain region contains the structures of the limbic system. The limbic system operates as our emotional brain and includes the amygdala, a small structure responsible for more intense emotional states (e.g. rage). Various brain structures and chemical processes are responsible for feelings of shame and reactions to trauma. Researchers have been studying the brain activity of emotions for generations.

The bodily reactions of shame have been studied as far back as Charles Darwin in the 1870s. In his 1992 book, *Shame, the Exposed Self,* Michael Lewis reports on Darwin's observations. He relays that Darwin explained shame as emotion that can be expressed and seen via facial expression and through the specific movements of the head and body. Darwin proposed that by observing facial muscles around the eyes and mouth, one could identify the primary emotions of happiness, fear, and anger. It is interesting that Darwin also observed that the emotion of shame is an expression experienced throughout the entire body, rather than only on the face. Darwin proposed, "When one is shamed, the head is averted or bent down with the eyes wavering or turned away (what is now referred to as gaze avert). Darwin noted facial blushing is a manifestation of shame, and he also pointed out the reddening of the skin, the bringing of blood vessels to the surface, takes place not only in the facial region but all over the body." [33]

Psychological Components of Shame

Shame is considered a self-conscious emotion, beginning with the internal process of self-awareness, self-introspection, and self-reflection. From these self-evaluations, one begins to make self-attributions (the manner in which individuals explain the cause of behavior and events). These self-attributes can be corrective, disparaging, or any combination of the two. When the experience of shame deepens, it leads to a matrix of self-devaluation, negative self-imagery, and yields self-hatred and self-loathing; it simply becomes an attack on the self. Shame is a complicated emotion that occurs on multiple levels of mental experience.

---

33   Lewis, 1992

Conceptually, shame is often misunderstood. The terms 'guilt' and 'shame' have often been mistakenly used interchangeably. Researchers all the way back to the 1970s, such as H.B. Lewis in his book *Shame and Guilt in Neurosis* (1971), encouraged a differentiation between the two emotions, especially for the purpose of theory and measurement. Other researchers have attempted to define guilt and shame. Their works have defined *guilt* as an unpleasant emotion accompanied by a belief one should have thought, felt, or acted differently. They defined *shame* as an unpleasant emotion accompanied by a global negative evaluation of the entire self, characterized by internal self-doubt and chastisement.[34,35] One can surmise from these definitions that shame is a much more personal and often debilitating emotion than guilt. Schalkwijk writes that shame is a powerful, generally negative self-conscious emotion associated with the internal evaluation of the self or identity, whereas guilt comes from the external, where a person examines how they compare according to some outside standard or rule.[36]

We have all experienced guilt for wrongdoings, and each circumstance contains a component of guilt and shame. We have been involved in events, thoughts, or actions that have left us questioning our intentions, our worth, and ultimately, ourselves. At times, this shame can be overwhelming — able to engulf our psyche with feelings of self-loathing and despair.

Surprisingly, research proposes shame can impact an individual in both negative and positive ways. While some research has proposed shame has been empirically linked to psychological maladjustment and is positively correlated with suspiciousness, resentment, irritability, self-

---

34   Kubany & Watson, 2003
35   Tangney, 1996
36   Schalkwijk, 2008

oriented personal distress reactions, anger, and externalization,[37,38] other theorists have proposed shame plays an important role in the development of our moral compass.[39,40] The conflicting results show how much more research is needed to truly determine the long-lasting effects of shame on an individual.

Sigmund Freud described a human's personality structure as a triune entity consisting of our Id, Ego, and Superego. Our Id is the hedonistic, pleasure-driven part of us. Its counterpart is the Superego, functioning as the parental portion that monitors and controls the many unfiltered impulses introduced by the Id. It is the job of the Ego to function as a conductor, orchestrating a balance between our wants, desires, and needs. Without the presence of guilt and shame, we could easily be consumed by the destructive power of the Id. Shame is often a result of the energy required to restrict, or allow, the hedonistic drives and impulses of the Id. Within the Freudian model, shame has a purpose.

Parental roles in shame development

How does this all relate to creating shame in children? Children enter this world vulnerable to their environment, parents, and other adults. The child is dependent for food, water, shelter, and nurturance. The significance of a parent cannot be underestimated, as they are the life-source for the child: the foundation for physical, cognitive, emotional, spiritual, sexual, and moral development. Parenting styles contribute greatly to the manner in which a child learns to balance the Id, Ego, and Superego, and how shame will be experienced.

---

37 Tangey, 1991
38 Tangney, Wagner, Fletcher, & Gramzow, 1992
39 Eisenberg, 2000
40 Tangney, 1991; 1992

Pia Melody writes, "Children learn to self-esteem first from their major caregivers. But dysfunctional caregivers give their children verbally and nonverbally, the message that the children are 'less-than' people. The 'less than message' from caregivers becomes part of the child's own opinion of himself or herself. Upon reaching adulthood, it is almost impossible for those raised with the 'less-than message' to be able to generate the feeling from within that they have value." [41]

For Ben, the "messages" were confusing. He lacked messages from male role models and his child-mind had to extrapolate meaning from this absence. He felt a sense of abandonment and struggled to build a framework for proper father-son interaction and a foundation for gender development and identity. At an extremely young age, the abandonment of a parent can start the "merry-go-round" of shame, which can eventually turn into toxic shame. Claudia Black, Ph.D, renowned addiction specialist and noted author of *Changing Course* writes,

> Not receiving the necessary psychological or physiological protection equals abandonment. And, living with repeated abandonment experiences creates shame. Shame arises from the painful messages implied in abandonment: 'you are not important. You are not of value.' Unresolved pain of the past and pain in the present created by past-driven behaviors fuel our fear of abandonment and shame. [42]

Ben's mother also contributed to the "mixed messages" being delivered to Ben's psyche. Sometimes, she was extremely loving and caring, even to the point of over-indulgence. By overcompensating for the lack of a male role model in her son's life, she caused Ben to cling to his mother

---

41   Melody, 1989
42   Black, 1993

for an abnormal number of years. At times, he felt emotionally responsible for her as the enmeshment grew exponentially.

Object Relations is a theory of personality development that is based upon the attachment style a child has to its primary care giver. Object Relation theorists would say Ben did not appropriately "separate-individuate", meaning he did not understand where his mother's identity ended and his identity began. Furthermore, as previously discussed in detail, he also received unhealthy and confusing messages about being a "boy" but was frequently allowed to exhibit behaviors more stereotypically consistent with being a "girl". This introduced even more occasion for confusion and made him further question his self-worth. Claudia Black describes this experience, saying, "When children experience chronic abandonment with distorted boundaries, they live in fear and doubt about their worth."[43]

Self-esteem and self-worth develop at early ages. Even as early as the age of 3, children begin to evaluate their competency and ability to navigate the world. They explore whether it is safe to venture away from their parents and then run back to home base for security. This is how Object-Relations theorists propose children learn separation-individuation and develop their personal boundaries. Children want to do things independently, such as dress themselves, pick out their own meal, pour their own drink, and make decisions for themselves. How a parent interacts with the child during this developmental stage, allowing the child to interact with the world while gently guiding them and encouraging increased independence, is an integral part of the child's developing sense of self.

It is imperative to know that what a parent says becomes the inner voice of the child. It is of vital importance that caregivers are extremely careful

---

43   Black, 1993

with the manner in which they address their children. If a child hears harsh, descriptive words such as "stupid", "ugly", or "mean" directed towards them, these words have the potential to become the internalized descriptors they repeat to themselves, aiding in the destruction of their own self-concept.

> Over the years, given our experiences, we have developed a committee of internal voices that have become our Inner Critic, telling ourselves we are stupid, not wanted, ugly, and unimportant; this is in response to any slight or perceived loss, or when we feel slighted by someone we value.[44]

The critical words Ben heard from his internal voice in his younger years was like a T-shirt he wore on a daily basis. They were continuously with him, telling him he was not good enough; he wasn't boyish enough; people hated him because he was a "sissy"; and many more unfair and demeaning statements.

Parents are not the only source of influence on a child's developing sense of self. Children interact with other people within and outside of the nuclear family. As parents, it is important to carefully consider whom you expose your children to and how those individuals interact with your child.

The incident with Ben and the two girls on the school bus exploring the physical difference between boys and girls, and the resulting actions of the aunt who found out, is an example of outside influence. Jeannie's aunt made Ben feel shame. Her sense of disdain for the situation left him feeling not only guilty that he had violated some standard of conduct, but shame was communicated through her body language and

---

44   Black, 1993

facial expressions. As stated earlier, this may have been the first time he became aware that he had disappointed adults in his life and maybe even God himself. Though his behavior needed to be redirected, his curiosity was age-appropriate. Children are naturally curious about the differences between the sexes and reasonably try to grasp concepts of biological sex, sex roles, and the underpinnings of gender identity. It is important that this curiosity isn't shamed. Ben's mother did not over-react to the event and provided him with appropriate information about boundaries for future behavior. Her response was a form of correction and redirection, as opposed to shaming. Ben perceived that Jeannie's aunt, on the other hand, had a negative emotional reaction regarding what he had done. He remembers her speaking with her hand placed over her heart, and the look on her face communicated a combination of disgust and disappointment coupled with a degree of horror. This reaction induced personal shame, leaving him believing not only was his behavior inappropriate, but he, himself, was a bad person because of the bus event.

As a child grows, it is imperative that parents are the main source of teaching, correcting, nurturance, and support. A child must be given a strong foundation of self-esteem and self-worth, so when others induce shame and bad messages, there's a greater chance of those bad messages being challenged and filtered versus immediately internalized. Children encounter many people throughout their lives such as teachers, coaches, bosses, etc., who have the potential to induce shame and cause emotional damage. When they are provided with a strong foundation, the child can appropriately process shame from others and can hopefully avoid "toxic shame", which will be explored later in this book.

CASE EXAMPLE

Shame can originate from many different sources and can be intergenerational, as previously discussed. Shame can be passed down from parents, turning into a multigenerational shame spiral. For example, Gary is a 44-year-old Caucasian male who owns a successful heating and cooling company and is well known within his community. He drives a large Dodge Ram truck and dresses in tight shirts, which enhance his muscular physique. He's played football since the time he was a toddler. Gary's father, the local high school football coach, reared Gary in close proximity to other athletic males and the team locker room. Unbeknownst to anyone, Gary has always felt insecure and has thus overcompensated with dramatic displays of masculinity as evidenced by his truck, occupation, bulging muscles, excessive drinking, and bragging. Gary always felt he could never live up to the athletic expectations of his father who would dote on the players he coached. Though he longed for the acceptance of his father, Gary rarely received it.

Gary is now the assistant coach of the local junior high football league. His own son, Josh, now 13 years old, is on the field dressed in cleats, shoulder pads, and a jersey. Gary stands on the sidelines and screams at Josh when he makes a mistake like not running fast enough or fumbling the ball. Gary's youngest son, Paulie, is on the sidelines being given orders to do push-ups, sit-ups, and other "tough guy exercises" at the young age of 6. Gary proclaims his family will have a "pro-football player, one way or another." Paulie frantically performs the exercises and constantly seeks his father's approval. Meanwhile, Josh is on the field playing the game, but is consumed with emotional pain. He knows he cannot meet the unrealistic standards his father imposes on him and feels guilt and shame for not living up to his father's expectations. Josh is also deeply concerned that Paulie will someday be the professional football player, winning all of their dad's attention, and he will ultimately lose any approval he has with his father. Josh is hurting for his younger brother and the anticipated shame Paulie will feel that mimics Josh's own. Josh is angry with his father for treating his little brother this way. The boys are living within a multigenerational shame spiral that continues to regenerate throughout this family, leaving the males insecure, angry, and immature. Because males in these types of situations are taught to be "tough" and aren't allowed to show emotions, the transmitted shame has little chance of being openly addressed and is likely to continue from one generation to another.

Male Shame Development

William Pollack's and Ronald Levant's compilation, *A New Psychology of Men*, includes a chapter written by Dr. Steven Krugman entitled "Male Development and the Shame Transformation". During this, Krugman proposes that shame plays a significant, but unspoken, role in the life of men and that all men have a deep personal knowledge of shame and work diligently to conceal its presence. He proposes that shame can come in the form of being teased for playing with girls' toys and for being a 'chicken' to do something seen as masculine. Shame "becomes the companion of every soldier who, facing battle, dreads his own terror and the possibility that his unmanly fear will cause him to act like a coward." Krugman discusses the competitive, insensitive, and often cruelness of boyhood. Events such as being chosen last, not being chosen at all, being picked on, being afraid to fight, or forced to fight all create intense feelings of shame. Then, in adolescence and adulthood, males face fears and shame about penis size, sexual functioning, and fears of sexual stamina and premature ejaculation. He also writes,

> Shame signals vulnerability, difference, exposure, and loss of control. When the process of shame socialization is adaptive, boys learn how to manage themselves in relation to authority, peers, and intimate others. But when it is disrupted by developmental and gender role pressures or by psychological trauma, males have a particularly difficult time integrating shame-based experience.[45]

Krugman also cites Pleck, who proposed men experience sex role strain, which involves attempts to adhere to rigid, narrow gender norms from a traditional ideal of masculinity. However, the author admits every man has the human experience of feeling inadequate, inferior, needy, and insecure.[46] When men and boys feel these things, they are left with the sense that they do not measure up or do not fit in with what is expected from their gender, resulting in shame. So often, this shame remains hidden and is never shared. Too often, it is numbed with alcohol and drugs, forgotten during sordid sexual escapades, quieted during an all-night gambling spree, or drowned out by the rage of a violent domestic altercation. Those in pain find any avenue they can to hide and escape from underlying shame; however, many of those choices come with additional consequences that breed further shame and guilt.

---

45   Pollack & Levant, 1998
46   Ibid

Alpha males and non-alpha males

For the purposes of this book, we will assume that male gender scripts follow two primary paths: the alpha male (AM) script and the non-alpha male (N-AM) script. By definition, the alpha male (AM) is considered to be one who learns and attempts to emulate the society-driven, narrow definition of masculinity. Chapter 11 further discusses the "Man Rules" of being an AM. The AM maintains a tight reign on his emotions, giving off a "tough guy" image that does not allow for any signs of sensitivity and weakness. Emotions are either ignored completely or released in the form of anger and aggression. The AM's focus is often on athleticism or some other form of "masculine" competitive activity such as hunting. An example of a high school AM would be the "jock" who plays sports and is praised primarily for his athletic ability. In adult life, the AM is often the man who limits emotional expression, sees clear delineations between the roles and responsibilities of men and women, and has a traditionally masculine occupation.

The non-alpha male (N-AM) usually follows a less traditional definition of masculinity and tends to be more sensitive. He is in touch with a range of emotional experiences, allowing him to experience emotions individually and genuinely, without filtering them through a more dominant emotion such as anger. The N-AM may enjoy activities that are creative or artistic, such as writing or listening to music, or other activities not thought of as traditionally male-oriented. The N-AM may be challenged in his athletic abilities and may enjoy more intellectual or talent-driven endeavors. These men are also more likely to experience issues with gender role conflict. It is important to note that gender role conflict is not necessarily linked to sexual orientation. Most N-AMs are equally as heterosexually oriented as the AMs. It is possible the experience of gender role conflict may contribute to a N-AM's sexual identity formation; however, the internal questioning of sexuality is often possibly a result of male peer rejection and ridicule rather than a homosexual orientation.

While researching this book's material, I would often share with friends and colleagues that I was studying N-AMs' experiences of gender role conflict and their correlation with toxic shame, complex trauma, and unhealthy behaviors in men. Surprisingly, many of the AMs I shared this with added their own stories of how they, too, have experienced gender role conflict, or how they have been hurt by the expected "male code of conduct", which resulted in underlying toxic shame.

Many men expressed how challenging and traumatic it was for them to maintain the level of masculinity required by AM societal expectations. They discussed the social pressure they felt and the degree of insecurity with which they struggled while attempting to maintain the stereotypical cultural standards of 'masculinity'. They discussed the emotional experiences they have been deprived of by not allowing themselves to fully feel and express their emotions, often avoiding vulnerability in their intimate relationships. Based on these testimonials, it appears both the alpha and non-alpha males have challenges based upon the narrow, rigid cultural definition of masculinity.

Even though the majority of this book is written with the N-AM in mind, I want to give credit to all men who experience varying degrees of gender role conflict, emotional pain, shame experiences, and who struggle with society's expected code of masculine conduct. Our male struggle is real, difficult, and can be painful. We are not alone, and trauma for men is real: trauma from absent or uninvolved fathers, bullying, shame, abuse of all types, and having to navigate a world in which the definition of masculinity is narrow, with a norm that does not appreciate all types of men.

SELF-REFLECTION QUESTIONS

1. *What are your definitions of shame and guilt?*

2. *In what ways have you experienced shame?*

3. *How would you describe your relationship with each of your parents?*

4. *What did your parents provide to you emotionally, physically, and spiritually? What did they not provide to you?*

5. *What shame-inducing memories stand out about your childhood?*

6. *Can you identify any patterns of multigenerational shame in your family?*

7. *If you are a man, do you consider yourself an AM or a N-AM?*

8. *What characteristics of each can you identify within yourself?*

9. *What emotions do you feel uncomfortable expressing as a male?*

10. *What pressures do you feel from living in an AM driven society?*

08 | BULLYING

*"What if the kid you bullied at school,
grew up, and turned out to be the
only surgeon who could save your life?"*

— Lynette Mather

Gone

One pivotal Saturday morning during Ben's first grade year, he awoke to find an open space in his closet where his Barbie airplane cabin and dolls had previously been. He confronted his mother and asked her, "Mom, where is my Barbie airplane and my Barbie stuff?" Nothing could have prepared him for her response.

"I gave them to Sarah, they are gone, Ben. Boys don't play with Barbie dolls."

He felt numb and dumbstruck: Did he believe what he had heard? He was shocked and confused. "Sarah, who is Sarah?" he asked.

"It's your friend Eric's little sister," she said. He suddenly pictured her in his mind and knew who she was. He visualized how during his trips to Eric's house to play cars, he would have to watch Sarah play with his other set of favorite toys.

Now, as an adult recalling this day, he wishes there had been some discussion about what was happening. Specifically, why was it suddenly no longer appropriate for him to play with Barbie dolls? He felt betrayed, as if there was a family secret kept from him concerning the inappropriateness of his playthings.

As an adult, he discussed that Saturday with his mother. When he questioned her about the decision to give his toys away, she stated she believed his interest in Barbie dolls was merely because he wanted to play with his sister and her friends. But now that his sister was no longer interested in the dolls and he seemed to be becoming more engaged with his two male friends, she thought it would be no problem to pass the Barbie dolls along. He asked his mother why she had not told him of her plan, and she said she often would purge toys she felt he and his sister were no longer interested in; this time is was the Barbies. Unfortunately, she did not understand the strong attachment he had formed to those beloved toys.

Though his mother believed she had been acting in his best interest, Ben's young mind could not make sense of what was happening. He asked if she was concerned about his interest in playing with them even after his sister was no longer interested. She replied that she thought it was normal 'kid stuff' and she simply thought that he liked his cars more now. She did not realize that he was deeply attached to the cross-gendered toys.

I would advise parents who need to intervene in their child's life in matters that are beyond the child's cognitive reasoning abilities to speak to them about the situation at an age-appropriate level and with language they will understand. Children are truly just little humans with the ability to think and feel. The simple act of sincere communication can let a child know that you care and have their best interest in mind, even if they dislike your actions or decisions.

Ben's life changed drastically the day he woke up to find his Barbies given away. This was the day he began to think he was not normal. If his mother had gone to such extreme measures as to take away his toys and give them to someone else, surely something must be deeply wrong with him. Shame hit young Ben in waves, beginning an emotional cycle that he carried well into his adult years.

Throughout the rest of that year and for years to come, he contemplated what was wrong with him and where he fit in. He thought, "I am male; I am a boy; what does that mean?" Before, he had thought he was simply Ben, an individual with certain tastes and affinities; but now he deeply believed there was something wrong with him because he was a 'boy' who liked dolls. He was not prepared for the immediate fall-out at school because of his mother's intervention with the toys.

Eric and Sarah's brother, David, was three years older than Ben. He did not care for either of the boys and found great satisfaction in teasing them. David would make fun of them for playing even with the more stereotypical masculine cars and would often call them names like "little sissy" and "girl".

After that pivotal moment in which his toys had been given to Sarah, he knew David had an even greater reason to torment him. David now knew that Ben had played with Barbie dolls, as they had been handed down to his younger sister, Sarah. Ben knew there would be a heavy price to pay now that the older boy was aware of his affinity for dolls, and he was correct. It was a hell that lasted more than 10 years.

David went to his fourth-grade class and told everyone about the Barbie collection: how it had been taken away from Ben and given to his own young sister. David started to relentlessly torment Ben at school, calling him names like "sissy", "faggot", and "girl". Other boys started to pick on Ben, pushing him, wanting to fight him, and demanding that he "prove" he was a boy. Ben cowered and withdrew; he could not have fought, nor did he *want* to fight them.

He soon became the laughing stock of Cameron Elementary School. Children can be incredibly cruel to one another, and Ben found himself ostracized and alone. Being picked last in P.E. class felt like a form of torture to the young, vulnerable boy; no one wanted a "faggot" who didn't know the rules of the game on their team. He began to dread school with a great passion. This would be the case for most of his elementary, junior high, and high school years.

The trauma of being bullied penetrates deep into a child's psyche. Nothing can prepare an innocent child for the cruelty of being bullied. The trauma of bullying during his school years left deep scars that changed the course of Ben's life in many devastating ways. The pain from the bullying brewed inside him torturously.

He felt his insides collapsing, breaking down, and he wanted to disintegrate. He didn't want to live. He didn't know what this was called, but he felt he wanted to die rather than live with this pain. Looking back, he didn't know a first grader could experience suicidal ideation but was able to interpret and identify it as an adult. Though he was only a child, his misery was real and he found himself considering ways to end his young life.

For the next 20 years, he frequently fantasized and obsessed over suicide. He considered many different ways to end his life. His upbringing and conservative belief in the eternal consequences of suicide (namely, that it would "send you to hell for eternity") were his only defense against committing the act. These two concepts, of wanting to die, yet being afraid of an eternity in hell, left him at a crossroads. He wanted to be dead but did not want to pay the eternal price associated with suicide.

The Trauma of Bullying

Bullying, especially repeated bullying, can be extremely damaging to the psyche of a child, and I believe that it can even lead to complex trauma. It is a form of peer abuse that can cause deep scars and pain. Often, the bullied child unconsciously retains the voices of those who are taunting him or her and will continue hearing the hurtful phrases and degradation long after the actual perpetrators have left, so they, in a way, become their own bully. The child's own inner voice and psyche betray him, repeating the mantra of his peers.

CASE EXAMPLE

To help underscore the dramatic and devastating life-long effects bullying can have on an individual, I will share one man's experiences with you. Rex is in his 40s and now sits in my office, attempting to work through his childhood bullying trauma. Many painful memories emerge from his childhood and adolescence. As a child, Rex was small in stature and not very gifted athletically. As a fairly quiet kid, he struggled to socialize with other boys. He recalls being in a physical education class during which he felt uncomfortable, as he was athletically rather uncoordinated and untalented. The P.E. teacher was not sympathetic to Rex's lack of physical ability, and even went so far on one occasion as to hit Rex upside the head with a basketball on purpose. The other boys in the class erupted in laughter. Naturally, Rex felt humiliated by the teacher's blatant attack and felt incredibly embarrassed as he considered how the P.E. teacher could do this to him in front of the entire class.

Rex's P.E. horrors only worsened. Many of the football players were in Rex's gym class and would often taunt and bully him. One afternoon, when P.E. class was over and it was time to shower, three of the football players approached Rex in the locker room. Two grabbed him by the arms, forcing him to his knees, while the third taunted Rex about "liking penis" before taking out his own penis and rubbing it all over Rex's face. The same P.E. teacher sat in his office in front of a large picture window facing the locker room, and did nothing to stop the assault or to assist Rex. The adult who was responsible for the class and Rex's safety had clearly abandoned him, allowing the bullying to occur.

Rex dealt with a third incident of severe bullying during gym when these same boys shoved him into a set of folded-up bleachers, dislocating his shoulder. Again, the teacher never intervened.

The shame, humiliation, and embarrassment of these three incidents have haunted Rex well into his 40s, as he now processes the extent of his trauma. At my practice, I have seen countless people with experiences like Rex, who are wounded from the experience of bullying 20, 30, or even 40 years after the events have taken place.

Being bullied was the single most traumatizing aspect of Ben's childhood as well. It left scars that affected him for years until he consciously decided that he would no longer be bound by his pain.

If you have been a victim of bullying, do you ever fantasize about confronting your bullies now that you are an adult? Do you ever wonder what you would say and how you would confront them? Do you desire revenge and want to hurt them, bully them, or seek retribution for what they did to you? If so, rest assured, as these are all normal thoughts for a bullying victim. I was recently visiting with a friend and discussing the development of this book, and we began a discussion about bullying. He relayed a story about his recent 25th high school class reunion. He approached a man he recognized and reached out his hand to greet his fellow classmate. Instantly, the gentleman said, "No you don't. Get away from me. I don't even want to talk to you: you were one of those guys who teased me." My friend was shocked at what the man had to say. He remembered, on at least one occasion, teasing the man in class along with some other friends. He attempted to tell the man it was all only in fun and on that day, even he had been laughing and joking with them about it. My friend had no idea that his behavior had hurt the man so deeply. Upon realizing the trauma that had occurred, my friend profusely apologized and asked the man for forgiveness. Unfortunately, the man had no interest in the apology or granting forgiveness and making amends. It is sad, yet important, to realize that individuals who experience bullying carry the wounds with them for many years.

The Impact of Bullying

According to the U.S. Department of Health and Human Services' (DHHS) anti-bullying website, **stopbullying.gov**, bullying is defined as intentionally aggressive, usually repeated verbal, social, or physical behavior aimed at a specific person or group of people. Some bullying actions are considered criminal, such as harassment or hazing, but bullying alone is not an illegal activity. Recent news stories abound with tales of cyberbullying. This is a type of bullying where the target is harassed through social media or other technology and has resulted in many victims' suicides. The site reports as many as 43 percent of students have been bullied online.[47] While there has definitely been an increase in cyberbullying, much bullying still takes place at school. In fact, as many as one in three U.S.[48] students say they have been bullied at school. The site shows an analysis of the research statistics concerning bullying, determining that most students who are bullied are seen as "different" from their peers. The students most likely to be bullied are those who are special needs; Lesbian, Gay, Bisexual and Transgendered (LGBT); overweight; and/or perceived as "weak" by their peer group.

The Center for Disease Control reports that according to studies conducted in 2008 and 2010 by Yale University, bullied victims are two to nine times more likely to consider suicide than those who have not been bullied.[49] In his book, *Shame: The Exposed Self*, Michael Lewis proposes "suicide is likely to be the result of shame associated with rage directed inward." Lewis also says, "Rage is a response to prolonged shaming."[50] A victim of bullying experiences a high degree of shame but has nowhere

47   "What is Cyberbullying", 2018
48   Ibid
49   Kim & Leventhal, 2008
50   Lewis, 1992

to dispel the shame. This is the "freeze" response or the immobilization that occurs in the brain when a child cannot escape the bullying. Eventually, the shame manifests itself as rage, and the person turns against him or herself, leading to a suicide attempt or suicide completion.

Bullying and Suicide

According to the Centers for Disease Control and Prevention (CDC), suicide is the third leading cause of death among young people with approximately 4,400 deaths every year. The CDC estimates at least 100 suicide attempts occur for every one suicide among young people. As of 2015, more than 14 percent of high school students have considered suicide and nearly seven percent have attempted it.[51]

In an interview with Fox 6 TV News on May 28, 2015, Daniel Brigg's mother told her son's story which soon went viral. Daniel had been bullied for most of his life. She reported the bullying intensified during high school because the New York native did not like sports but preferred hunting and trapping. Daniel was called names, had trash thrown at him, was punched, was made to lick a bus window, and was ridiculed for the music he listened to. The mother reported that Daniel received a text from one of his bullying peers that stated, "Why don't you take one of your precious guns and do the world a favor and go kill yourself?" Daniel replied, "You won't have to worry about me anymore, I'm going to go home and kill myself." In response, he received a text saying, "Put up or shut up." Daniel had told many people at school that day he was going to kill himself and even told the bus driver at the end of the day he wouldn't see him anymore. Unfortunately, Daniel was serious about his threats and tragically ended his life that day. Looking at Daniel's picture

51   "Bullying and Suicide", n.d.

you can see he was a "boy's boy" and he liked gender stereotypical activities of hunting and trapping, but because he did not fit the Jock stereotype according to masculine ideology, he was not accepted and had to struggle with a life of taunting and teasing. This is another of many sad examples of how bullying leads to toxic shame and complex trauma that could ultimately result in suicide.

Many others have faced similar struggles. Ronin Shimizu was a sixth grader at Folsom Middle School, in Folsom, California. Ronin was the only male cheerleader on his school's squad and was bullied as a result. He, too, committed suicide. Ryan Halligan was bullied due to his learning disorders, passion for music (guitar and drums), and his love for theater. Ryan hanged himself at the age of 13. There was an unnamed 7-year-old in my beloved home city of Detroit who hanged himself with a belt from his bunk bed because he was constantly teased at school for being the only boy in a home of eight females.

Transgender teens are at a high risk of bullying and suicide. Eleven identified transgender teens took their lives in 2015. A few of those are as follows: Kyler Prescott, 14 year-old, an accomplished pianist, activist for marriage equality and animal rights committed suicide on May 18, 2015; Josh Alcorn, 17-year-old from Ohio; Cameron Lagrell, 15-year-old from Racine, Wisconsin; Taylor Aleena, 16-year-old from San Diego, California; Blake Brockington, 18-year-old from Charlotte, North Caolina; Leela Alcon, 17-year-old from Union Township, Ohio; Zander Mahaffer, 15-year-old from Georgia; and Melonie Rose, 19-year-old from Maryland.

As an adult and therapist, I understand that children who bully most often are suffering from their own emotional and mental pain and are stuck in their own shame spiral. What has happened to them that drove them to project their shame emotions onto others? What makes them identify with their own aggressor and inflict pain upon others? Simply put, their emotional needs are not being met. By building a reputation as a bully, they have found a form of social acceptance and a unique place of strength in the social pyramid of the schoolyard. The cliché that "negative attention is better than no attention at all" is often proven in these sad bully-victim situations.

SELF-REFLECTION QUESTIONS

1. *Were you ever bullied?*

2. *If so, for what?*

3. *Do you still 'hear' the voices of the bullying in your head?*

4. *Have you internalized those messages to become your self-talk?*

5. *Have you ever been the bully?*

6. *If so, what were the underlying emotions causing you to bully?*

7. *How do you think the person you bullied felt and what impact did it have?*

8. *Have you ever thought of making amends with this person?*

9. *Has your life been impacted by suicide?*

10. *Have you ever had, or do you still have suicidal thoughts?*

11. *What are your feelings and internal reactions to the teen suicides that were mentioned?*

12. *Have you ever thought of confronting your bully? If so, what would you say? If not, why not?*

13. *What would you be looking for from the bully? What would be your expected outcome?*

09

TOXIC SHAME

> *"Shame needs three things to grow exponentially in our lives: secrecy, silence and judgment."*

> — Brene Brown

Carl Jung, one of the world's most respected and quoted psychiatrists wrote, "Shame is a soul-eating emotion." I have to agree with him. Shame grows like a cancer and breaks down the fibers of the soul. In her book, *Facing Codependency*, Pia Melody says, "Hug your demons or they will bite you in the ass, if you do not embrace what is dysfunctional, you are doomed to repeat it and stay in the pain."[52] Another phrase that is common in recovery circles is, "you're only as sick as your secrets." All of these phrases hold immense truth. These state-

---

ments identify how shame has great, potentially destructive power in our lives if left unchallenged and unresolved. Unhealthy levels of shame must not be hidden in the psyche, but exposed and resolved, allowing the healthy self to blossom.

One of the goals of this book is to examine the role of toxic shame and its destructive power. For Ben, toxic shame was birthed from several issues: Absent Father syndrome, Father Hunger, an over-compensating mother, and gender role conflict. Together, these wreaked havoc on his emotional and mental development.

Why is shame such a powerful influence for some people? There has been a vast amount of research examining how and why certain individuals are more prone to feelings of shame than others. Those who are more prone to shame are more likely to experience pervasive problems in thinking and behavior due to that shame. Frank Schalkwijk writes about those who experience shame in a disproportionate measure to the shame-inducing event:

> In most extreme cases, feeling ashamed has become a prominent aspect of emotional regulation, meaning that this personality trait has permeated the individual's entire emotional life. In some individuals, this interplay is so powerful that it brings about pathological shame at a toxic level.[53]

The term "toxic shame", allegedly coined by Sylvan Tomkins in the 1960s, is the experience of shame beyond what is related to behavior — it is shame of who you are as a person. This toxic shame can become a child's mantra, their inner voice, and, eventually, their identity. This can happen to individuals more prone to shame emotions, or those who

---

53   Schalkwijk, 2008

have experienced deep shame from a traumatic event, ongoing trauma, or abuse. Similarly, Rizzuto wrote about "pathological shame", proposing that pathological shame is usually not related to actual events or temporary thoughts or fantasies but is "associated with unconscious, long-standing convictions and unconscious fantasies about negative self-esteem; inadequacy and not being worthy of love."[54] Both Tomkins and Rizzuto describe shame that is defined by how one identifies oneself, separate and distinct from the actual shame-inducing event. Both recognize the impact of shame that deepens to a detrimental level at which the person's self-beliefs become toxic in themselves.

To use an analogy, when an insect builds a cocoon, it takes layers and layers of silk and other material collected to form a hard exterior shell. Toxic shame becomes layers of a child's cocoon, engulfing, enveloping, and swallowing the beauty of the true self that lies within the child. They may live in this cocoon of shame all of their life, never developing into the person they were genetically and existentially designed to become.

I have had clients say they've heard things such as, "I should have worn a condom when I had sex with your mother." Parents do not always understand the damage they can cause by telling kids, "you were an accident" or "we wanted a girl." These statements cause a child to question their worth as a human being and cause them to feel unwanted, believing their very existence is not valued. Toxic shame can develop when a parent denigrates the inherent worth of the child. The message of "I am defective" plays over and over and contributes layers and layers of trauma.

Once toxic shame sets in, it easily leads to depression. Aaron Beck, a famous Cognitive-Behavioral Psychologist, proposed the theory of the

---

54   Rizzuto, 2008

Cognitive Triad to explain depression. The triad is comprised of three components: Worthlessness (I am no good); Helplessness (there is nothing I can do about this); and Hopelessness (I will always be this way). Toxic shame leads one to feelings of worthlessness, helplessness, and hopelessness resulting in depression. Abiding toxic shame attacks the self on every level.

I recall sitting in therapy with a man named Reid, who identified as a Christian and admittedly had a problematic relationship with pornography. As a conservative Christian young man, Reid had been socially awkward. He had not dated much through high school or in college. Eventually, he started attending a small church where he met Lisa and they married within a few months. Neither had dated much prior to that, nor had they had any previous sexual experience. Lisa experienced Postpartum Depression after the birth of each of their children, leaving Reid without sexual intimacy for many months. Eventually, he began viewing pornography and masturbating on a regular basis. Each time he would view pornography and relieve himself, he was flooded with waves of overwhelming guilt and shame and would beg God for forgiveness. The negative voices in his head were so full of self-hatred and self-loathing, his shame developed into toxic shame. Eventually, his wife discovered his sexual secret, only deepening Reid's shame spiral. During this time, he also received a diagnosis of diabetes. He soon ended up in a counseling office, convinced God had given him diabetes as a punishment for his horrendous sexual sin. In his mind, he had become an awful person and God was punishing him. In Reid's case, toxic shame did not originate from another person, but from within himself, as a result of his own interpretations of his behavior. Reid's toxic shame had induced irrational beliefs and emotions, as well as a significant degree of depression, as he believed that God could not love him and surely must punish him.

So, while shame originates from external sources such as in the cases of bullying or from internal self-rumination over one's personal decisions, toxic shame is birthed out of one's own interpretation of trauma or abuse. When feelings of shame are personalized and are identified within one's self-image and self-worth (often in the form of negative self-talk by the inner voice), the seeds of toxic shame grow, often leading to years of depression, self-depreciation, and ongoing trauma.

SELF-REFLECTION QUESTIONS

1. *What secrets are you holding on to?*

2. *Can you identify any shame in your life that has turned into toxic shame?*

3. *Where did toxic shame originate for you?*

4. *What does your toxic shame say to you?*
   What are your self-damaging messages?

5. *Have you considered seeking professional assistance to help you deal with your toxic shame experience?*

10

COMPLEX SHAME

*"The more elaborate his labyrinths,
the further from the sun his face."*

— Mikhail Naimy

As mentioned earlier, Dr. Lenore Terr described Type II trauma as a troubling event that occurs numerous times in a person's life. Francine Shapiro describes Small-t trauma as trauma that can happen again and again, creating an intermixing of emotions and cognitions that result in trauma. The recurring event (e.g. physical beatings or recurring humiliation) can synthesize into complex trauma. Serial trauma, with traumas occurring one right after another, can also compound into complex trauma. In the previous chapter, we discussed how shame can deepen until it develops into toxic shame, during which the psyche attacks itself with negativity and degradation. Complex trauma is the process of experiencing serial trauma, causing exponential layers of emotional pain which deepens the level of toxic shame, often accompanied by simultaneous physical symptoms, such as PTSD reactions including nightmares, flashbacks, and dissociation, unhealthy conscious, and unconscious habits (i.e. continuing dangerous relationships), and many more diverse and undesirable symptoms. Essentially, complex trauma impacts every area of functioning, negatively affecting one's social, spiritual, emotional, behavioral, and familial dynamics.

When a child experiences ongoing shame and degradation due to gender role conflict or constant bullying as a result of deviation from the masculine ideology, a complex trauma can develop. The child falls into a constant state of alertness (hypervigilance) during which they are concerned about their behaviors, societal expectations, and ridicule from others. The child may have few places in life where safety is ensured and where they can be authentic. Eventually, the shame creates spontaneous, acute shame attacks and deepens into the toxic shame as discussed in the previous chapter.

Pia Melody speaks of these "shame attacks":

> I call an encounter with carried shame (*overwhelming shame*) a "shame attack." In a shame attack, you may feel as though your body is getting smaller. You may blush, want to disappear, run away, or crawl under your chair. It seems everyone is looking at you. Feeling nauseated, dizzy, or spacey is also common. You might start talking in a tiny childlike voice. And there is a tendency to "replay the scene" in your mind and let the shame feelings increase the next time through. In general, the experience of a shame attack is a dreadful sense of inadequacy.[55]

---

55   Melody, 1989

The fragile internal psyche of a child can only sustain so much repeated incongruence between their thoughts and behaviors, coupled with emotions such as fear, before complex trauma solidifies. Eventually, the child suffers emotionally and psychologically as life becomes a series of inescapable traumatic experiences.

Ongoing sexual abuse of a child is a poignant example that can be used to understand complex trauma. Blain was a third grader when his father died of a heart attack. His mother, with six children at home, quickly became overwhelmed with the demands of life. As is the case in many single-parent homes, his mother worked long hours to provide for the family. A few of the older siblings also went to work, helping the mother earn a living, so Blain was left with his older brother, Kyle, who cared for his daily needs. The family moved into an apartment where all the boys shared one room while the girls were in another. Many days after school, Blain would be forced to masturbate Kyle. With the new sleeping arrangements, Blain now slept in a full-size bed with Kyle, allowing his older brother easy access to Blain — not only after school, but also throughout the night. Kyle's sexual demands eventually progressed to oral sex or desiring to thrust his penis between Blain's tightly closed legs. Later on in counseling, Blain recounted the traumatic stories as they emerged from the recesses of his memory. He said, "I never thought to tell anyone. Everyone was so overwhelmed with my father's death and trying to put food on the table." At first, Blain would do anything within his power to resist Kyle, but he was still overpowered and forced to comply. Blain, remembering when the abuse would start, says,

> I somehow was able to separate my head from my body. I would let my mind drift off and go to various places where I was happy. I didn't allow my mind to return until I was relieved of the pressure from my brother's body.

As an adult, Blain now struggles with Post Traumatic Stress Disorder coupled with serious episodes of dissociation, which interfere with his occupation and family life. He will often lose time and "space out", becoming mentally absent from the present for several minutes at a time. Blain's trauma was repetitive and his mind created a method of survival over his powerlessness, and his recurrent sexual abuse formed into a complex trauma.

Ben's toxic shame that came as a result of continued bullying was what created his complex trauma. He remembers going to school fearful of what the day would hold. Countless times, he heard the words "sissy", "pussy", "faggot", "girl", or "wimp", or had to withstand the embarrassment of being the last person chosen on the kickball team. He hated himself and could not see any value or worth to his existence. Every day seemed to add a new layer of trauma. Day in and day out, the teasing was present, developing into a complex trauma as described in this chapter. Ben had no choice but to continue through the trauma, not recognizing it for what it truly was at the time. What happens to a child when trauma is repeated and inescapable?

The mind/body connection in humans is strong. Our central nervous system, consisting of our brain and spinal cord, is the conductor of the orchestra, creating music between our mind and body. Undoubtedly, trauma has deep psychological implications, as well as physiological and neural reactions in the body, that are extremely complicated.

Flight, Fight, or Freeze

Dr. Bessel van der Kolk is the founder and medical director of the Trauma Center in Brookline, Massachusetts. He is considered one of the world's leading experts in trauma and has studied the anatomy of trauma in the brain, experience, and in the lives of people. His recent book, *The Body Keeps The Score: Brain, Mind, and Body in the Healing of Trauma,* outlines cutting-edge research and practice guidelines for trauma. This book is full of rich information and I highly recommend it for patients and other professionals to educate themselves about the complicated concepts of trauma.

In the presence of trauma, the brain and body have three choices: flight, fight, or freeze. According to Dr. van der Kolk, "When the brain's alarm system is turned on, it automatically triggers pre-programmed physical escape plans in the oldest parts of the brain."[56] The oldest part of our brain, the brain stem, is considered the most primitive part of the brain. The brain stem is actively responsible for such essential bodily functions as breathing, heartbeat, and other automatic responses of self-preservation and protection.

Within his book, Dr. van der Kolk quotes work from Alessandra A. Lima's and associates research article entitled, "The Impact of Tonic Immobility Reaction on the Prognosis of Post-Traumatic Stress Disorder," published in the Journal of Psychiatry in March of 2010 where Lima reported,

> If for some reason the normal response is blocked — for example, when people are held down, trapped, or otherwise prevented from taking effective action, be it in a war-zone, a car accident, domestic violence, or a rape — the brain keeps secreting stress chemicals, and the brain's electrical circuits continue to fire in vain.

Long after the event has passed, the brain may continue to signal the body to escape a threat that no longer exists. Van Der Kolk expands this

---

56   van der Kolk, 2014

concept and suggests that, "Being able to move and do something to protect oneself is a critical factor in determining whether or not a horrible experience will leave long-lasting scars."[57] As was the case in Blain's story, his inability to escape from the molestation left him no choice but to learn the defense of dissociation. His abuse left long-lasting scars. The inner workings of his brain remained in "freeze mode" and long into adulthood, his brain continued to "freeze" with immobility whenever threatened.

Sometimes as a result of severe trauma, where the brain had to "freeze" to survive the trauma when escape was not possible, dissociation issues may occur. In simple terms, dissociation is an experience where the person blanks out, spaces out, or loses time. In other words, the person will be mentally absent from their present surroundings. Dissociation was how they endured the past trauma. Now, intrusive memories, flashbacks, or environmental triggers can alert the brain that a similar potential trauma is near. The individual will mentally disappear to escape the threat. Dissociation has no time limits. It can last from a few seconds to entire hours and range in severity. There are behavioral differences in dissociation, as well. Some individuals may sit and stare blankly into space, while others can continue movement and action, but not have a mental awareness of their surroundings or their behavior. A qualified therapist can help an individual struggling with dissociative states by teaching them grounding techniques, body awareness techniques, Emotional Freedom Techniques, Somatic Experiential Techniques, and mindfulness.

What about the child who is relentlessly bullied at school by other students? How can this child escape? "Flight" is not typically possible, as children are legally required to go to school. And meanwhile, the choice to "fight" bears with it several consequences ranging from personal physical harm to disciplinary results such as expulsion. However, there can be

---

57   van der Kolk, 2014

benefits to choosing to fight. While fighting, the body at least stays in motion and the brain can actively engage. Both body and brain are trying to protect the individual through physical offense and defense. If "fight" is possible, it can lead to potentially better outcomes than the other options. Often though, the only option available is "freeze." Many bullied children have no choice but to endure the abuse. They "freeze", trying to navigate internally through the layers of pain and resulting shame. Does this also lead to emotional immobilization where the child gives up the internal fight, accepting hatred, loathing, and unworthiness as a part of the experience of who they are? In today's technological environment that allows for social interaction 24/7, social media allows the torment to continue long after the school hours end in the form of cyberbullying. This ongoing trauma becomes complex as the victim's brain becomes stuck in a repetitive pattern, generating more self-hatred and self-loathing.

In good conscience, I must address a subject important to both me and other respected professionals in the psychological community: men have been underserved in understanding issues such as abuse, bullying, and the Small-t traumas which have been proposed by Shapiro in relation to trauma. Though the majority of the work concerning trauma started in the Veterans Administration with soldiers, the main focus of trauma research has focused around women. There is a current movement forging the exploration of trauma in men outside of war-related psychological wounding. I'm thankful for those researchers, such as Dr. Bessel van der Kolk, who are forging the study of trauma, and Dan Griffin, M.A., sociologist and author, who is applying research specifically to the lives of men in areas of recovery, relationships, and trauma. Chapter 11 will further explore Griffin's important work as it relates to "The Man Rules". For years, male sexual assault victims have been overlooked. The majority of the resources and programs for sexual abuse and assault are focused on females. There are far fewer studies, nearly non-existent in number, examining the impacts of verbal abuse, bullying, and other forms of social rejection and neglect on men and/or boys. Additionally, there is precious little research regarding the sexual abuse of boys by either men or women. I propose there is a gaping hole in academic research in this critical area that desperately needs to be filled.

Men are as susceptible to abuse, assault, neglect, and harm by words and behaviors as women. Many men not only go through their original traumas but are also secondarily traumatized by the lack of attention, research, and treatment offered to them and the fear of damage to their masculinity if they open up about their pain. Many forms of male trauma have the potential for reoccurrence with the vicious cycle created by poor access to healing resources. Complex trauma is real and happens to young boys, teenage males, and men, and it cannot continue to be overlooked. Victims must feel comfortable finding their voice; they must be heard; and the professional community is obligated to respond.

SELF-REFLECTION QUESTIONS

1. *Do you believe you are dealing with a complex trauma?*

2. *Have you identified the layers of your complex trauma?*

3. *Have you experienced cyber-bullying or witnessed it online?*

4. *How have you experienced fight, flight, or freeze during a traumatic experience?*

5. *Have you considered seeking professional assistance with your complex trauma?*

11

FINDING THE RULES

*"Guys, you don't have to act 'manly' to be
considered a man; you are a man, so just be yourself.
Don't let society make you believe you have to
prove your masculinity to anyone because you don't.
You are you, and you are worthy, full stop."*

— Miya Yamanouchi

How do boys learn to be boys? How do boys learn to become men? What is the code; what are the rules; when do you get your "man card"? In essence, what is the definition of masculinity? Psychologists and sociologists have examined these questions for decades. Researchers have been attempting to define male ideology since the 1970s. In the past, the definitions offered were extremely narrow and confining, not to mention harmful to the overall development of men. Some of the early researchers examined the "traditional male" ideology and identities of the American male.

In 1976, David and Brannon conducted one of the earliest examinations of American Masculinity. They described four standards of the traditional American masculinity:

(1) "No sissy stuff" - Distance self from femininity and emotions.
(2) "Be a big wheel" - Strive for achievement and success. Focus on competition.
(3) "Be a sturdy oak" - Avoid vulnerability, stay composed and in control. Be tough.
(4) "Give' em hell" - Act aggressively to become dominant.

If you were a male born in the 1960s or 1970s, you likely grew up adopting a mindset consistent with these four standards. Ben was a male born in the 1960s and grew up with these standards in place in society around him, but he never adhered to the standards and was not taught about them. Even though he was surrounded by the information, he failed to assimilate it into his identity either because he lacked a male role model or was ostracized by most boys in school.

The Boy Code

The process by which boys are exposed to these standards has been an area of study in the men and masculinity movement. William Pollack studied the exposure process, authoring the 1999 book, *Real Boys: Rescuing our Boys from the Myths of Boyhood*. In this book, he discusses The Boy Code, which, according to him, is the set of rules and expectations that come from outdated and highly dysfunctional gender stereotypes. In everyday life, The Code is both overt and subtle. Boys are not always consciously aware they are adhering to a code until they exhibit a violation of the code, and their peers quickly (and often viciously) inform them of their lack of conformance. Boys learn to live by The Code starting from a young age and allow it to guide their male journey into manhood where the rules are strictly enforced. In adulthood, when a man acts in a manner that resembles feminine behavior (such as expressing strong emotions like compassion, sadness, or fear), they are said to have "lost their man card." This is a cliché term that generally implies that they have broken the Boy Code.

> The Boy Code continues to affect the behavior of us all — the boys themselves, their parents, their teachers, and society as a whole. None of us is immune — it is so ingrained. The Boy Code puts boys and men into a gender straight-jacket that constraints not only them but everyone else, reducing us all as human beings, and eventually making us strangers to ourselves and to one another - or, at least, not as strongly connected to one another as we long to be.[58]

Pollack also proposed the concept of "gender straight-jacketing" in which Caucasian Euro-American culture shames boys toward extremes of self-containment, toughness, and separation from nurturing caregivers.[59] Pollack states that boys are likely to take these standards and critically judge themselves internally. They may even be judged by others and surmise they are immature, underdeveloped, deficient, and fail to pass the test of masculinity.

The Man Rules

Sociologist Dan Griffin has worked with men and recovery for the past 20 years. In his book, *A Man's Way Through Relationships*, he exam-

---

58   Pollack, 1999
59   Ibid

ines the development of men and boys and the concept of masculinity by a careful dissection of what he calls "The Man Rules." These are expected rules offered by society that men adhere to both consciously and unconsciously.

Griffin proposes that many "Man Rules" are communicated to boys throughout their lives. Some of the rules are spoken and are well-known, whereas others are unconscious messages coming from numerous sources. The Man Rules, Griffin writes,

> are unwritten, yet very real, and they guide our lives from an early age, telling us how to be boys and men. We follow these Rules to let the world know we are real boys and real men. When we don't follow them, we run the risk of being viewed by others and viewing ourselves as being less than *real* boys or men.[60]

Griffin proposes some of the most common Man Rules are:

- Don't be weak;
- Don't show emotion;
- Don't ask for help;
- Don't cry; and
- Don't care about relationships.

According to Griffin,

> The Rules at their extremes are toxic. They lead to disconnection, violence, homophobia, objectification of women, and extreme competition, as well as isolation, loneliness, self-hatred, and misery... Practically from the moment we are born, men are raised with messages conflicting with those given to girls and women.

---

60   Griffin, 2014

We receive messages — explicitly and implicitly — not only are certain behaviors against the Rules, they are to be avoided because they are associated with the 'weaker' sex.[61]

For generations, men have stifled behaviors and the expressions of emotion out of fear of appearing weak. It is common for men to come to my office and discuss their marital problems. Their wives complain about their lack of emotions and their inability to express real intimacy or connection. The women complain that their men "are out of touch with their emotions." Unfortunately, many of these men have learned from a young age, through The Code or Rules, to run from emotions out of fear of breaking the masculinity code that they are forced to live by.

Men, in their quest for masculinity, often feel they cannot risk learning how to foster connection with another individual. They are taught to avoid looking weak; therefore, they avoid expression of most emotions, with the exception of anger, and the careful attention to a relationship that may make one appear weak. Men often relate to one another in more superficial ways: limiting their conversation to a few socially acceptable topics such as sports, cars, or their jobs.

I find it strange that men generally make sweeping assumptions about one another and their interests, like assuming most, if not all, men enjoy and follow sports. I was recently at a social event at which a new, casual acquaintance started our conversation by asking, "What's your favorite football team?" to which I replied with my usual, "I hate football" response. He continued with: "Basketball? Baseball? Soccer?" to which I replied, "Quite honestly, I don't like sports at all." I made an attempt to change the conversation to something more relevant to our current setting and situation, but he eventually turned and walked away. Having little idea how to interact with me, he felt most comfortable leaving the conversation. I couldn't help but think about The Man Rules and this person's inability to interact with me. The Man Rules had clearly affected his emotional maturation and his ability to interact with more non-traditional males.

Men have followed The Boy Code or The Man Rules so unconsciously they are not even aware of the synthetic nature of these predilections, strictly adhering to them to their own detriment. Boys grow up in a world with expectations about their strength, mannerisms, and prowess, and develop into men that carry on these unhealthy traditions. These men face great struggles in their intimate relationship with others, especially their partners and children. These processes are so easily learned and ingrained, with most men not questioning the developmental process and the possible misinformation that they have integrated into their idea of manhood. Other men may be aware that they break The Man Rules but will go to great lengths to conceal it. To illustrate, I would like you to consider the experiences of Bradley.

Bradley, a man in his mid-30s, is happily married with a beautiful daughter. He is an intelligent, athletically built man, with a successful career, and even speaks a few different languages. Though he has a strong masculine presence, Bradley maintains a secret. As a youth, he was a competitive figure skater at the national level. At some point, Bradley moved on from this sport and pursued other interests; however, he admittedly chooses not to share his history with others. He recognizes the potential for scrutiny by other men and stated, "To this day, I still don't tell people about it due to the gender-identified nature of the sport." Bradley is adhering to The Man Rules and hiding an important part of his history that undoubtedly was meaningful to him. His competitive skating was likely a strong influence on the successful and driven person he is today.

As exemplified in Bradley's situation, the socially embraced Man Rules are confining, and often cause men to deny healthy parts of themselves that could possibly inhibit connectedness to other males.

Ronald Levant, Ed.D. is a pioneer in the study of men's psychology. He has written numerous journal articles, and some of the most quoted and well-known books in the field. Throughout his works, he has examined the traditional beliefs of the American male and examined many aspects of the male ideology. He summarized the traditional American masculinity into seven principals:

(1) Restrict emotions;

(2) Avoid being feminine;

(3) Focus on toughness and aggression;

(4) Be self-reliant;

(5) Make achievement the top priority;

(6) Be non-relational and objectify sex; and

(7) Be homophobic. [62]

Dr. Levant has studied how men view themselves in relation to these seven principles. He and his colleagues developed The Male Role Norms Inventory. A short form can be found online at www.drronaldlevant. com/mrni.html. The site allows you to answer questions and provides you with a summary of results. The results inform you how strongly you adhere to the seven principles. I would encourage each of my male readers to take the test and examine your masculine ideology. More than likely, you are following some degree of The Man Rules whether consciously or unconsciously. Examine how your adherence to the Rules might be interfering with your ability to live fully.

---

62   Levant et al., 1992

In conclusion of our examination of The Man Rules, I leave you with Dan Griffin's thoughts. He writes, "Some men have learned the hard way that when they do not follow The Rules, they are made fun of or rejected for not being manly enough, not only by men in their lives, but by women as well." He goes on to propose that boys feel safer from the criticism and harshness of peers the earlier he learns to follow The Man Rules. Boys often learn The Man Rules in a violent fashion from other boys. Griffin also proposes this process of socialization can cause a male to separate from core parts of his humanity, thus giving every man at least some degree of trauma.[63]

SELF-REFLECTION QUESTIONS

1. *Which of David and Brannon's four standards do you most identify with?*

2. *What was your Boy Code?*

3. *What was/are your Man Rules?*

4. *How did you learn The Boy Code/Man Rules?*

5. *Which of the rules do you currently believe?*

6. *How do you think the rules have affected your life? Relationships? Work?*

63   Griffin, 2014

12 | SOCIETY'S MESSAGE

*"In a society that tries
to standardize thinking,
individuality is not highly prized."*

— Alex Grey

Both men and women fall prey to society's messages about The Man Rules. Both sexes are victims of the unconscious absorption of the all-encompassing and ever-present gender role information provided by their environment. Society has a strong message regarding men and masculinity that is portrayed throughout a man's lifespan, beginning as soon as his mind starts comprehending the provided messages. As a toddler, children start receiving societal messages via television. The messages continue through school, textbooks, cinema, video games, social clubs, social networks, sports, and many other diverse avenues.

Researchers Lorriane Evans, Ph.D, University of Georgia and Kimberly Davies Ph.D., Augusta State University conducted a study in which they examined the fictional characters within elementary school textbooks and discovered the male characters were consistently more aggressive, argumentative, and competitive.[64] What message is this sending to young readers about how their behavior depicts their masculinity? Children internalize the message that being tough, aggressive, argumentative, and competitive is the way to be male and how to display masculinity. Citing the work of Ellexis Boyle Ph.D, social researcher regarding media representations, and Sean Brayton Ph.D, researcher and expert of popular culture and film and television (2012),[65] and Jeffery A. Brown, Ph.D, researcher of gender and body issues in film,[66] Robert J. Zeglin, author of "Portrayals of Masculinity: Aging masculinities and 'muscle work' in Hollywood Action", investigated masculinity within Hollywood movies and found it to be portrayed through labor capacity (a man's ability to work), physicality and muscularity (physical condition), heterosexuality, a tough poise, and sadomasochistic themes (infliction of pain on others).

Men in Romance Novels

In a 2013 article written by Jonathan Allan in the Journal of Men's Studies, the role of masculinity and the "hero" in romance novels was examined. He cites a well-known study titled, "Reading the Romance", by author Janice Radway in which she describes the male body in popular romance novels to be a site of "spectacular masculinity", and writes "every aspect of [the hero's] being, whether his body, his face, or his

---

64   Evans and Davies, 2000
65   Boyle and Brayton, 2012
66   Brown, 2002

general demeanor is informed by his maleness."[67] Another researcher in this area, Tania Modleski writes, the hero is "a handsome, strong, experienced, wealthy man."[68] History has laid the foundation for this type of thinking and writing. In his book *Stigma*, sociologist Ervin Goffman described the American male as "young, married, urban, northern, heterosexual, Protestant father of college education, fully employed, of good complexion, weight and height, and a recent record in sports." He goes on to say, "any male who fails to qualify in any of these ways is likely to view himself — during moments at least — as unworthy, incomplete, [and] inferior."[69]

Romance novels often focus on the physique of the male hero character. An examination of the male body in romance literature is described as "slim, toned, and muscular".[70] A study conducted by Murray Drummond examined the "archetypal heterosexual male body" and writes "it is one that is muscular, but not too muscular. It is a body that is devoid of fat and hair. It must be that one is 'cut' and 'chiseled' and it must appear strong and powerful."[71] Romance novel authors typically describe the male hero in their stories as wealthy, strong, powerful, manly, authoritative, intelligent, charming, mysterious, valiant, and protective; yet somewhere, amongst all of these excessively masculine traits, the hero is also able to understand and be entangled with the emotions of his conquest, as he relates with her on the deepest level.

The descriptors worsen as these authors describe the male body with terms such as flat stomach, rigid, six-pack abs, hard muscular chest, bulging biceps, trim, firm, narrow hips, broad shoulders, tight skin, strength,

---

67   Radway, 1984
68   Modleski, 2008
69   Goffman, 1963
70   Gill, Henwood, & McLean, 2003
71   Drummond, 2011

lean torso, tan, long powerful legs, hairless chest, and rippling muscles. These become even more masculine and farfetched during sex scenes, in which the author employs words such as throbbing, aching, bulging, pulsating, straining, length, heat, swollen, and virile. In these novels, men use women for their pleasure, and the women beg for more. Men become erotic objects of fantasy. Read one of these novels and you will see that men are objectified within these books as much as women are in heterosexual pornography. How ridiculous and unrealistic is this stereotype of the hero and the ideal body of a man? Few men fit this ideal image being portrayed to the many women reading romance novels. I contend that romance novels, with the erroneous portrayal and objectification of men, are as harmful to a woman's internalized ideal of the opposite sex as pornography is to a man's. And yet, we hear little, if anything, about the effects of this on relationships and their outcomes.

Men in Pornography

The pornography industry, which grew exponentially in the 1980s, only makes matters worse. With the advent of the internet, people gained access to free pornography whenever they desired. In my work, I regularly counsel teenaged boys and college-aged young men, most of whom watch pornography. Studies have shown the average age at which kids are first exposed to pornographic images online is 11 years old.[72] Pornography has become commonplace in today's culture, with seemingly a large majority of teenage boys and men admitting they have watched, occasionally watch, or watch porn on a regular basis. Research has produced varying results in attempts to find the largest group of internet pornography consumers by age. It is also difficult for researchers

---

72   Ropelato, 2014

to ascertain averages concerning the number of times a teenage boys accesses internet pornography in a week and the average amount of time spent on porn websites.

Many boys I have seen for therapy have reported that they only watch porn for 10 to 15 minutes, using it as an avenue for masturbation. Other boys will admit to spending several hours perusing multiple videos and genres of porn before achieving sexual gratification. I have also heard college-aged males report that watching pornography is an easier avenue to meet their sexual needs than having to make a true connection with a female, worry about being rejected, or having to spend time and money maintaining a relationship. These same college-aged males admit they have watched enough pornography that they are now experiencing sexual problems in the form of erectile dysfunction and/or delayed ejaculation (difficulty or inability to ejaculate after a sustained period of sexual intercourse). Thus, entering into a relationship with a female is now embarrassing and fearful.

Pornography brings more self-deprecation than release to the males who are watching. Not only do the men in pornography often exemplify the rare physique described in romance novels, but their actual manhood is exposed and open to evaluation. Many porn actors report that the industry standards require the male porn star's penis to be at least 7.5 inches, if not 8 in length or larger, when erect; the male actor must be able to achieve an erection on command and maintain it for long periods of time, have the ability to control his ejaculation until the director calls for it, and be able to become erect again within minutes.[73,74] Actual research from reputable journals such as *The Journal of Urology* and *The Journal of Sexual Medicine* have reported that the average penis size for adult males

---

73   Miharia, 2017
74   Ora, 2016

has ranged from 5.1 to 5.6 inches in length.[75,76,77] Fisch's book, *The New Naked: The Ultimate Sex Education for Grown Ups*, reports statistics from previous studies recording the average sex act as 7.3 minutes in duration, but an astonishing 43 percent of such acts are completed within two minutes.[78] Though statistics vary greatly, it is important to understand that pornography creates false expectations for young, susceptible boys, teens, and men who are trying to figure out how to be a male in our culture. Pornography gives them the wrong perceptions of their bodies, their penis, their sexual capabilities and expectations, and what to expect from women during sex. It also eradicates the concept of true sexual and personal intimacy, as most pornography is purely lust-driven and animalistic in nature. What message is this sending the males who watch porn on a regular basis? It saddens me to think of the damaged self-esteem that the average male faces while inevitably comparing himself to the unrealistic standards propagated by pornography. We, as men, struggle greatly with the society's verbal and non-verbal Man Rules, and now men are demeaning themselves further by subjecting themselves to pornography, making comparisons, and coming up short, mentally and physically.

In addition to the harmful effects pornography has on the adolescent male's self image, the current education system also can detrimentally affect a young man's sense of self-worth. Social Psychologist Phillip Zimbardo, Ph.D stated that "young men are not failing at school: the school system is failing them." Some of the issues he reports as problematic for boys are elimination of recess and gym class; reading requirements being set before the boys' brains are developed and ready for this

75   Wessells, Lue & McAninch, 1996
76   Sengezer, Ozturk & Deveci, 2002
77   Herbenick, Reece, Schick & Sanders, 2014
78   Fisch, 2014

task; and the lack of hands-on learning activities (where boys have been proven to excel), which most classrooms are not set up for. Another detriment for boys in school is that fewer than one in nine schoolteachers are male. Overall, these issues put boys at a disadvantage in the classroom.[79] In his book, *Real Boys: Rescuing our boys from the myths of boyhood*, William Pollack, Ph.D, discussed the idea that boys were falling behind in public schools and the academic system was not properly addressing their needs. Girls were outscoring boys in many areas, and boys were failing to develop healthy aspirations for the future. Boys were also falling behind in their academic skills and had low motivation for successful careers. According to Pollack, boys struggle more with their self-esteem than girls do and tend to have a lower self-image. I believe these issues, identified by Pollack in 1999 and studied again by Zimbardo in 2012, illustrate that the education environment for males has worsened with time and continues on a frightening trajectory, threatening the mental welfare of developing male students.

The Man Rules and Women

The Man Rules impact women as well. These unconscious messages are internalized by the female psyche, affecting a woman's perception of and behavior towards men. We can see this in the example of my client, Don, and his family.

---

79   Zimbardo, 2012

CASE EXAMPLE

Don, during his weekly session right after the Christmas holidays, is slightly disturbed about an event that occurred over the holidays. Don is not an alpha male: he is an art teacher and enjoys painting, decorating, and cooking. He does not like sports and is more attuned to his emotions than the average man. Don is married, heterosexual, and has three sons. His brother, Joe, is a masculine, gay male who enjoys traditionally masculine activities, especially riding dirt bikes and four-wheelers. Don relates to me that when Joe decided to inform their mother he was gay, she looked at Don and said, "I always thought it would be you." Don, good-naturedly, laughed at this.

Don's sister, Lisa, habitually gives both Don and Joe more feminine gifts at Christmas. The brothers often laugh about how feminine the gifts are but, this particular year, Lisa gave him a white ceramic Christmas tree with holes in it where you place candles to light, as well as a print of a lady dressed in a lacy Victorian dress walking down a snowy path away from the viewer. Don was puzzled at her choice of gifts for him. He stated he felt the gift was more appropriate for a 60-year-old woman. Don, being embarrassed about the gift, felt awkward opening it in front of the family. Deciding he had reached his limit, he let Lisa know how he felt about the gift selection. She was apologetic, saying she had never realized she gave her brothers feminine gifts.

Stereotypes are powerful for both sexes. Don's mother assumed he would be homosexual because he did not like sports and was more interested in the arts. The sister gave her brothers feminine gifts because one was a gay male and one was not a traditional alpha male. It appears both women were unconsciously engaging in stereotypic behavior, channeling a stereotype they did not even recognize.

How many times do others unconsciously perpetuate this belief that a non-alpha male is feminine or even potentially gay? It is often implied in our culture's messages to the extreme. The portrayal of men in romance novels, movies, media and pornography are often heavily exaggerated and unrealistic, sending a pervasive message that, if you are a man who is sensitive, caring, or enjoys activities considered less masculine, you must be a homosexual; and vice versa: if you are a homosexual, you must be less masculine.

We, as men, must learn to broaden our definition of masculinity and learn to be more accepting of one another. Our individual likes and dislikes have nothing to do with sexual preference. Men need the freedom to focus on being human and experiencing life with a full range of emotions and activities without fear of judgment or relegation. Men must learn to be themselves — not what Hollywood, romance novels, or porn wants you to be. It is perfectly acceptable for men to be sensitive, emotional, and cry at sad or happy things. I remember crying at my wedding while my wife was smiling the entire time, only shedding a few tears. I remember being overcome with emotion at having found acceptance in a beautiful woman who loved me and did not put barriers on my masculinity. She allowed me to be myself: the person I was and am today.

SELF-REFLECTION QUESTIONS

1. *What is your definition of a man?*

2. *What adjectives would you use to describe being a man?*

3. *How do you feel about the way men are portrayed in TV, movies, and various forms of media?*

4. *What is your reaction to how men are portrayed in romance novels?*

5. *What are your feelings about the ideal male body type?*

6. *How do you feel about your body?*

7. *Do you think boys are at a disadvantage in the educational system?*

13

GENDER CONFLICT AND CONFUSION

"Gender is like a Rubik's Cube with 100 squares per side, and every time you twist it to take a look at another angle, you make it that much harder a puzzle to solve."

— Sam Killermann

In second grade, more confusing messages filled Ben's head. Though no longer playing with Barbie dolls, he loved the Super Friends League of Justice. He watched Linda Carter play the role of Wonder Woman every Friday at 7 p.m. She was gorgeous. Ben convinced his mother to buy him a Wonder Woman lunch box to carry to school. And, of course, he was made fun of for the stereotypical feminine choice.

That Halloween, his school was going to have a Halloween parade and march down the town's sidewalks. Ben wanted to be a witch that year, so his mother, being a great seamstress, made him a witch's robe and hat, and found a wig for him to wear.

Ben didn't understand why it was OK for him to carry a Wonder Woman lunch box and to dress like a witch at Halloween, but not OK to play with Barbie dolls. The gender rules seemed so arbitrary — he honestly didn't know what he could and could not do. It seemed like, no matter what he did, he was made fun of. The trauma continued, layer upon layer. Ben was being smothered by complex trauma.

This was the age at which Ben began to mentally self-examine more intently. Boys are supposed to like certain things, but he didn't like those things. Girls are supposed to like other things, but he liked more "girl things" than "boy things". He tended to be more sensitive, caring about the feelings of others, and what happened to them. He could never have said or done the things that the bullies said and did to him. He wondered if there had been a mistake. Was he meant to be girl instead of a boy? Nothing seemed to be right for him in this boy body and boy life.

The internal thoughts he had as a child were consistent with a phenomenon called Gender Role Conflict. Gender Role Conflict is defined as a "psychological state in which socialized gender roles have negative consequences on the person or others." Individuals can experience gender role conflict in their thoughts, emotions, behaviors, and even on subconscious and unconscious levels of mental functioning. Research studies show that men tend to experience negative consequences concerning themselves and in society due to struggling with gender role conflicts.[80] Researchers C. D. Thompkins, C. Durham, and R.A. Rando examined 343 males from a Midwest urban university. They found that the more

---

80   O'Neil, Good, & Holmes, 1995

gender role conflict an individual experiences, the more shame that person experiences in their life.[81]

Further research examines the concept of role theory. It is thought that gender roles and gender stereotypes emerge from observations of the typical social roles of the sexes. Through these observations, an individual assumes that other people's social behaviors usually correspond to their inner dispositions.[82,83] How many boys try to fulfill a role based on their social observation, even if it is not congruent with who they are? Yet out of fear of being punished or demeaned, they acquiesce to the expected role. Consider the boy who watches wrestling, believing he must be physically aggressive to be accepted as a boy; however, this boy is small in stature and does not have the physique to intimidate his peers. Consequently, he will act tough and may even be willing to put himself in danger by acting aggressively. This is an example of gender role observation affecting one's inner disposition and associated actions.

Usually between the ages of 2 and 3 a child can answer the question, "Are you a boy or a girl?" Yet, they still cannot conceptualize what this truly means. A person's core gender, their inner sense of being male or female, is usually established by age.[84,85] According to Jean Piaget, a pioneer in the work of child development, a 3-year-old child is still in the pre-operational stage of development, meaning that they only identify gender based on manifested content such as clothing and hairstyle. The child's understanding that gender remains permanent does not tend to form until age 6 or 7. It is also at this stage that children start to recognize that genitals are a major factor with regard to gender. Therefore, the

---

81   Thompkins, Durham, & Rando, 2003
82   Eagley & Steffen, 1984
83   Hoffman & Hurst, 1990
84   Kalbfleisch & Cody, 1995
85   Gallagher & Kaufman, 1995

typical child begins their gender formation based on cues such as clothing, hairstyle, toys, genitals, and how their parents refer to them. Once the foundation is laid, the child starts to solidify their gender identity.

Gender Identity Development

What process do children use to identify and solidify their gender identity? Various researchers have proposed different steps. Carol Lynn Martin, Ph.D. and Diane Ruble, Ph.D., professors and researchers in the areas of socialization and development, conceptualize the process into three stages:

> (1) as toddlers and preschoolers (age 3 to 4), children learn about defined characteristics, which are socialized aspects of gender;
>
> (2) around the ages of 5 to 7, identity is consolidated and becomes rigid;
>
> (3) after this "peak of rigidity," fluidity returns and socially defined gender roles relax somewhat. [86]

Barbara Newman, Ph.D., author of *Development Through Life: A Psychosocial Approach*, breaks gender identity formation down into the following four components:

> (1) understanding the concept of gender;
> (2) learning gender role standards and stereotypes;
> (3) identifying with parents; and
> (4) forming gender preference.

---

86   Martin and Ruble, 2004

It is possible that during any of these stages, gender role conflict may emerge. A child may have identified their gender and started their developmental journey, but individualistic desires may conflict with specified gender expectations, resulting in a gender role conflict.[87]

To further understand gender role conflict, let's examine the work of Joseph Pleck Ph.D., author of *Men and Masculinity*, and Jim O'Neil, Ph.D., editor of *A New Psychology of Men* and author of *Men's Gender Role Conflict*. The definitions of terms they utilize will help the reader digest the following content. O'Neil defines devaluations, restrictions, and violations in the following manner:

> *Devaluations* - "Gender role devaluations are negative critiques of self or others when conforming to, deviating from, or violating stereotypic gender role norms of masculinity ideology. Devaluations result in lessening of personal status, stature, or positive regard."

> *Restrictions* - "Gender role restrictions occur when confining others or oneself to stereotypic norms of masculinity ideology. Restrictions result in controlling people's behavior, limiting one's personal potential, and decreasing human freedom."

> *Violations* - "Gender role violations result from harming oneself, harming others, or being harmed by others when deviating from or conforming to gender role norms of masculinity ideology. To be violated is to be victimized and abused, causing psychological and physical pain." [88]

---

87   Newman, 2015
88   O'Neil, 2008

Gender role conflict

Pleck proposed men experience gender role conflict directly or indirectly in six contexts:

1. Deviation or violation of gender role norms;
2. Attempts to meet or failure to meet gender role norms of masculinity;
3. Experience discrepancies between their real self-concept and their ideal self-concept, based on gender role stereotypes;
4. Personal devaluations, restrictions, or violations;
5. Experience personal devaluations, restrictions, or violations from others; and
6. Personally devalue, restrict, or violate others because of gender role stereotypes. [89]

Additionally, O'Neil separates gender role conflict into four different types, as shown below.

O'Neil's first three types of conflict help quantify and elaborate upon Pleck's previously mentioned contexts (especially 4, 5, and 6):

1. **Gender Role Conflict Within the Man:** the private experience of one's negative emotions and thoughts experienced as gender role devaluations, restrictions, and violations.

2. **Gender Role Conflict Expressed Toward Others:** Men's expressed gender role problems that potentially devalue, restrict, or violate another person.

---

89   Pleck, 1981

3. **Gender Role Conflict Experienced From Others:** Men's interpersonal experience of gender role conflict from people interacted with that results in being personally devalued, restricted, or violated.

4. **Gender Role Conflict Experienced from Role Transitions:** Gender role transitions are events in a man's gender role development that alter or challenge his gender role self-assumptions and consequently produce gender role conflict or positive life changes.[90]

It is inevitable that males will experience some degree of gender role conflict through one of the four types proposed by O'Neil. Boys will accidentally do something that does not conform to the gender rules. They will recognize this deviation and devalue themselves, or someone else will recognize the behavior and point out the violation. And, as a result, boys quickly learn to restrict their behavior in order to avoid devaluations and violations.

In today's world, gender information has become confusing for many. The media focus on transgender issues and individuals, with such high-profile examples like Caitlyn Jenner, has only added confusion to the topic. It is easy to confuse transgender issues with the construct of gender role conflict, when, in actuality, transgender issues are only one form of gender role conflict. Gender role conflict occurs on a continuum from the subtle to the more acute. Gender role conflict can serve as an overarching umbrella with many aspects of the experience found beneath it. When a male experiences gender role conflict, it has nothing to do with your specific gender identification or sexual orientation. Gender role conflict does not necessarily have any correlation with sexual iden-

---

tification, whether that be gay, straight, bisexual, bicurious, or any other varied form.

Society now has many terms regarding the concept of gender: i.e., gender queer, gender fluid, gender variant, gender non-conforming, etc. These individuals, who identify themselves similarly, do not identify as either male or female. They tend to believe the gender concept lies somewhere along a continuum, falling somewhere between many possible points. Or, they may consider themselves fluid on this continuum, moving between one gender or the other depending upon current feeling. Some also see their gender as continually evolving and changing. Transgender individuals believe that they are internally the opposite sexed gender, and some go on to seek sex-reassignment surgery to make their internal and external sex congruent.

Gender dysphoria

At times, children can become confused about their gender. When this occurs, the child is experiencing Gender Dysphoria, or what some researchers refer to as "extreme gender nonconforming behavior." Previously, this was known as Gender Identity Disorder.

Gender Dysphoria, as it is outlined in the *Diagnostic and Statistical Manual of Mental Disorders V,* [91] is a strong and persistent feeling of cross-gender identification. The child must have six or more of the following for at least a six-month period:

- Repeatedly stated desire to be, or insistence that he or she is, the other sex;

---

91   American Psychiatric Publishing, 2013

- In boys, preference for cross-dressing or simulating female attire; in girls, insistence on wearing only stereotypical masculine clothing;
- Strong and persistent preferences for cross-sex roles in make-believe play or persistent fantasies of being the other sex;
- A strong rejection of the toys/games typically played by one's sex;
- Intense desire to participate in the stereotypical games and pastimes of the other sex;
- Strong preference for playmates of the other sex;
- A strong dislike of one's sexual anatomy; and/or
- A strong desire for the primary (e.g. penis, vagina) or secondary (e.g. menstruation) sex characteristics of the other gender.

CASE EXAMPLE

Let's take a look again at John from Chapter 4. John spent his earlier years modeling the behaviors of his mother and avoiding his hurtful father before experiencing trauma at the hand of a family friend who told John, "You would make a good girl." After hearing this, John ruminated upon this idea. He recalled playing 'house' or pretending he and his friends and/or cousins were the characters from the television show, *Happy Days*, when he would often choose to play the role of a female character. He remembers during his early teen years when he decided to dress up like a woman for Halloween. Increasing his deepening trauma, he recalled hearing several people remark that he would have made a great girl. This only made him further question his gender. He admitted to occasions when he had dressed up in his mother's clothes — filling her bras with water balloons, adding padding to his underwear in order to smooth out his crotch, thereby appearing more feminine. In his mind, though, he also admired the *Star Wars* character, *Han Solo*, describing him as masculine and rogue — doing what he wanted to and not caring what others thought. John desired to be like Han Solo: masculine, strong, and potent. However, people's comments about his sensitivity and emotionality, feminizing him with their responses, started him on a journey of questioning his gender identity. If evaluated at that time, John would have met the criteria for a clinical diagnosis of Gender Dysphoria. It was only later in life when John was able to work out his gender and sexual confusion and embrace himself as a heterosexual male who is sensitive, caring, and emotional.

Gender role conflict may be experienced by individuals who have no question about their gender, or by those who are in a state of flux about who they are and how to define themselves. As for Ben, he never met the clinical criteria for gender dysphoria. However, no one knew what was going on inside him; there was a definite internal struggle to understand his identity. He knew he was a boy and wanted to be a boy, but it often seemed as if life was fighting this endeavor. He didn't tell anyone how he felt, nor did he tell his parents about the bullying. He endured it and tried to fight through his problems on his own. Many children experiencing gender conflict or dysphoria suffer in silence, never revealing their torrid emotional experience. Researchers have attempted to examine the emotional experience of these children.

When a child feels they are violating the gender norms, an array of feelings can emerge. These feelings range from guilt, shame, anxiety, depression, sadness, and even panic. Various researchers have identified situations that elicit stress for men related to the violation of traditional gender roles,[92,93,94] such as being chosen last for the physical education activity due to a lack of athleticism or being made fun of in the locker room for having a delayed physical maturity compared to one's peers in regards to body muscle mass, presence of body hair, and maturing genitalia. These researchers also found that men typically reported stress in situations that reflect "physical inadequacy, emotional inexpressiveness, subordination to women, intellectual inferiority, and failure in meeting masculine standards of work and sexual adequacy."[95]

Additionally, researchers identified the negative psychological consequences of violating gender roles originates from both social disapproval and self-devaluation.[96] Because gender role norms are internalized at an early age, shame may also follow from failure to attain gender related ideals. Thus, violating these internalized gender role standards (i.e., deviating from what society defines as a "good" man or woman) may result in a direct threat to one's self-concept.[97] Andrew P. Morrison, Ph.D., author of *Shame: The Underside of Narcissism*, suggests gender role failure may lead to shame within individuals who evaluate themselves against masculine and feminine ideals and find themselves failing to meet those ideals. [98]

Ben and gender role conflict

To further illustrate how problematic emotional states are connected to gender role conflict, I will explain how Ben's gender role conflict developed into an anxiety disorder. He became an extremely anxious child,

92   Eisler & Blalock, 1991
93   Eisler & Skidmore, 1987
94   Gillespie & Eisler, 1992
95   Efthim, Kenney, & Mahalik, 2001
96   Ibid
97   Bem, 1987
98   Morrison, 1989

always conscious of his behavior, body movements, voice, and appearance. He became hypervigilant — over-analyzing and over-interpreting everything in the environment. Ben was constantly on guard for potential bullying, and his growing self-hatred and self-loathing was engulfing.

Ben's anxiety manifested itself as extreme tension that would often result in vomiting. He couldn't control the anxiety — its timing, intensity or duration. He had no way of stopping it, no matter how hard he tried, but his parents were becoming increasingly frustrated. They would ask, "What are you worrying so much about?" He couldn't tell them what was going on inside, for he was so confused and even he, himself, couldn't define his inner turmoil. Being in public with Ben was difficult for them, as he would vomit at the most inopportune times. He recalls vomiting often at night, lying in bed, as he worried about things far out of his control, eventually making himself sick. He specifically recalls being obsessed with the fear of being drafted into a war. He would think such thoughts as, "I am not a boy who can defend myself. I will surely die if I am ever called away to war. I am a weak, unmasculine guy. If the bullying is this bad at school, what would it be like in the military?" The rumination and vomiting episodes lasted intermittently for the next several years.

Ben's parents took him to a physician to discuss the anxiety and vomiting incidents. The doctor asked his parents to leave the room. He picked Ben up under his arms and sat him on a counter near a sink. Leaning over, he put his hands on the counter, one on each side of Ben, and stared directly into the young boy's eyes. He told Ben that he had control over this and that the only way he'd stop throwing up is if he decided to stop throwing up. It was all put on Ben to fix and control this.

Once again, he was receiving another message that he was broken in some way. The doctor became another adult male who failed Ben and didn't meet his needs. However, somehow this interaction gave Ben a sense of control and the courage to confront the chaotic emotions of his inner world that made him feel so helpless.

Boys experiencing gender role conflict need to feel a sense of empowerment and be told they have the skills to be effective in the world in which they live. Hopefully, this empowerment will come from his parents. However, it may come from other influential individuals in a child's life such as a mentor, doctor, or therapist. Many times, empowerment can be as simple as pointing a child in a safe direction in which he can express himself. Recently, while working with a client around Halloween, he explained that, this year, his young son, Jacob, wanted to dress up as Dora The Explorer. The parents were faced with a dilemma; though they were not bothered by the fact their son wanted to dress up as Dora, they were concerned about the potential social ramifications. Instead, the parents made a deal with the son that he could be Dora's friend, Diego. The son agreed and soon became excited about the character. I praised the client for handling this in an appropriate manner. The parents did not overreact to the situation, but considered the social implications and offered another choice to Jacob. I think this is an example of parents being open to their child's desires but also remaining cognizant of the current and future impacts of a child's decision. Were the parents restricting or protecting? I'm sure this could be open to argument and interpretation, but I believe the parents acted appropriately, with the child's best interests in mind. The parents empowered him with safe and helpful alternatives while still meeting his internal desires. And most importantly, they did not shame him for his initial desire to be Dora.

SELF-REFLECTION QUESTIONS

1. *How do you/did you experience Gender Role Conflict in your life?*

2. *What devaluations, restrictions, and violations have you experienced?*

3. *What negative outcomes have you experienced due to Gender Role Conflict?*

4. *What was your experience of shame as a result of Gender Role Conflict?*

5. *Have you ever known anyone with Gender Dysphoria or Gender Identity Disorder?*

6. *What was your reaction to this person?*

14

THE ARTICLE-PROPOSED ORIGINS OF GENDER ROLE, IDENTITY ISSUES, AND HOMOSEXUALITY

"Knowledge of self is the mother of all knowledge.
So it is incumbent on me to know myself,
to know it completely, to know its minutiae,
its characteristics, its subtleties, and its very atoms."

— Khalil Gibran

As a psychologist, I have worked with many who struggle with their gender and sexuality. I worked with Ashton from the time he was 17 until he was about 23. He was confused about his sexuality and was in conflict about how his homosexual tendencies were in opposition to his strong Catholic upbringing. He was unsure how to reconcile this dilemma.

During a therapy session, he brought in an article that had been written by Richard Fitzgibbons for Catholic Culture Library called "The Origins and Healing of Homosexual Attractions".[99] Although the article made no mention of being geared toward men (it simply used the term "adult"), most of the content seemed geared toward males and many of the examples provided are male. My client asked that I read the article over the coming week and be ready to process the content during our next session. I did so, and the article spoke volumes to me on both personal and professional levels.

In the article, Fitzgibbons proposes,

> The most common conflicts at different stages that predispose individuals to homosexual attractions and behavior are loneliness and sadness, mistrust and fear, profound feelings of inadequacy and lack of self-acceptance, narcissism, excessive anger, sexual abuse in childhood, and a lack of balance in one's life coupled with overwhelming feelings of responsibility.

The purpose of sharing this article with you is not to debate the origins, concepts or moral issues of homosexuality. Everyone must work out his or her own thoughts and feelings about this topic based on research and personal beliefs. I believe the article is worth examination for other reasons. I believe that the same theories about the foundation of homosexuality that are proposed by the author can be the same antecedents for gender role conflict. For now, I'll only discuss certain portions of the

---

99   Fitzgibbons, 2010

article. I will also add my own commentary, experience, and information shared by clients to help add context and interpretation.

I believe many factors contribute to gender role conflict, gender identity, and sexual identity development. Not one of these areas discussed can be applied to all individuals who are experiencing confusion or identity dilemmas.

Developing children and adolescents are often keenly aware of problems with social conformity. Many of these feelings lead to stress about not truly conforming to their assigned gender and their experience with gender role conflict. The examination of this article is for the sole purpose of examining how these areas might foster confusion for a child or adolescent whereas, if those variables were otherwise not present, the confusion may not have surfaced at all.

The first construct to be examined by the article is:

Sadness and Loneliness

Fitzgibbons suggests the most frequent cause of loneliness and sadness is the rejection that males can feel due to having limited or a lack of athletic ability during childhood and adolescence. Being athletically untalented often leads to hurtful criticism and rejection by a social network of peers. The pain a boy can experience by his lack of physicality can be significant. He may feel inferior when engaging in activities with boys who possess these skills and abilities, especially because these traits are so highly praised in our society.

Fitzgibbons also reports that approximately 40 percent of children and teens live in a home in which the father is not present. The absence of a father can also significantly contribute to a child's sense of sadness and loneliness, as we discussed at length in Chapter 3.

> When the need for warmth, approval, physical affection and praise from a father is not filled, an inner emptiness develops, often referred to today as 'Father Hunger.' In an attempt to overcome this pain, some adolescents and young adults seek comfort in being held by another male.[100]

This is not to imply that all boys who do not have a father figure, or did not get what they needed from a father, are going to develop some type of father issue, gender role conflict, or homosexual attraction. Still, boys who have a significant degree of loneliness and sadness, and lack athletic ability, and/or have experienced social rejection may be more likely to develop gender role conflict or some other type of gender or sexual confusion.

In my practice, when working with men who have "Father Hunger" or have experienced a "Father Wound", it is not uncommon for them to want to be held by a man to stave off the sadness and loneliness caused by the void left by men in their life. It is more acceptable for them to consider to themselves, "I might be homosexual", than to work through the pain of loss and abandonment. Many men go on to report, however, that lying in the arms of another man only abates the feeling for a time. The behavior does not prove to be a permanent corrective action for the sense of pain and abandonment that they experience by not having had a nurturing male figure in their childhood.

Having anonymous or casual sex with men can even become trauma repetition. Since it relieves the pain only temporarily, the pain returns

---

100   Fitzgibbons, 2010

in waves after the sexual encounter is over. The men repeat the pattern again and again, hoping for healing and a different resolution. Once some men are willing to face their underlying issues and recognize that their feelings come from trauma rather than sexual confusion, their desire to act out sexually often dissipates.

As previously stated several times in this book, anger tends to be the primary emotions expressed by males. Boys who experience sadness and loneliness may feel weak and have internal concern that these emotional experiences differ from those of other boys. This, too, can lead to gender role conflict.

Fear and Mistrust

According to Fitzgibbons, fear and mistrust originate from a male's inability to feel safe loving someone of the opposite sex is usually unconscious and originates most often from traumatic experiences within the home. In males this may be a consequence of having a mother who was overly controlling, excessively needy or dependent, angry and critical, unaffectionate and cold, narcissistic and insensitive, very mistrustful, and addicted or ill.[101]

Additionally, if a child is raised in a home with high conflict, it may result in the child growing up to fear heterosexual relationships, as their family model contained unhealthy physical and emotional boundaries. The child may develop the idea that this is the way all heterosexual relationships are, and he does not want to live through this ongoing pain in his own adult relationships.

---

101   Fitzgibbons, 2010

Fear and mistrust can be powerful forces. At times, hearing a client's story for the first time during a therapy session can be overwhelming. Nick came to me presenting the problem of sexual addiction with associated behaviors of cross-dressing and BDSM. BDSM is an acronym used for individuals whose sexual repertoire involves bondage and discipline/sadism (infliction of pain on others for sexual gratification) and masochism (sexual excitement experienced by pain). These behaviors and sexual desires were upsetting to both him and his spouse and were highly juxtaposed with his religious convictions. During my initial session with him, I found what he said alarming, as some of his behavior was dangerous and had the potential to be excruciatingly painful. I listened beyond the manifest content (what was being said) and examined the latent (underlying and hidden) content of what was being said, searching for the pain and message behind his stories. In Nick's story, I heard trauma that came from many different sources.

It took months of working with Nick to uncover the underlying origins driving his unhealthy behaviors. By providing him with a safe, non-judgmental place to talk, he eventually found the courage to tell his full story.

As a child, his family was exceptionally poor with few resources and lived a meager life. He often had to repeatedly wear the same clothes to school for days. As is the case with many kids of unfortunate means, he was severely bullied, which lead to a fragmented sense of self, coupled with an intense fear of the other kids. Nick reported that the other boys would follow him around and taunt him, saying they were going to get him and beat him up. Nick's fear intensified. He identified ways to escape the torture of the boys and started to secretly wish he had been born a female to escape the ridicule and criticism of the bullies. He figured that they would not treat him like this if he were a girl. At home, he found himself experimenting with cross-dressing, and often, while dressed as a female, he imagined himself walking, untroubled and without fear, home from school.

Another way Nick developed a sense of safety was by tying himself up with ropes and yarn and other materials of bondage and then trying to escape. He wanted to be fully prepared to play Houdini and skillfully free himself from any trap the boys may have prepared for him. He saw himself as a weak, helpless male, so he found a way to be empowered by preparing for capture and escape. Even though he had mastered some level of escapism, his masculine identity was suffering greatly.

Eventually puberty occurred. He experienced strong sexual urges and the surges of testosterone appropriate at that stage of life. These elements came together and caused a synergistic problem for which he was not prepared. He began mixing his cross-dressing and self-bondage with masturbation. The pairing of risky behavior with sexual arousal changes the brain's chemistry in the limbic system (the reward center) and can lead to sexual compulsivity, addiction, and/or deviance.[102]

Through the process of therapy, Nick gained insight into how the unwanted problem he was experiencing had come into existence. He was able to address the intense fear and trauma he still carried from his early childhood and unravel the problematic behaviors that had emerged in order to bring about healing.

Nick had no real desire to be female and did not truly suffer from sexual identity confusion, yet engaged in cross-dressing; this was distressing and bewildering to him. It was difficult for Nick to interpret this behavior as being related to anything other than gender identity confusion.

---

102   "Relevant Research and Article about the Studies", n.d.

Weak Masculine Identity

Some males grow up with strong feelings of inadequacy. According to Fitzgibbons,

> Self-esteem is based primarily on acceptance of the [parental] role model in early childhood ... Every male child yearns for acceptance, praise, and validation from his father in order to establish a positive sense of well-being and a degree of comfort with himself.[103]

No one is denying the need for a boy to also have the love of a nurturing mother, but there is a qualitative difference between the two. The positive influence of both parents is optimal.

If a boy grows up with a lack of acceptance by a father, it can lead to the child's inability to see himself as masculine; as a result, the child often feels weak and develops the impression that he could never please his father. Imagine a child who not only feels unacceptable to his father but is also ridiculed by his peer group for being athletically untalented, as we discussed previously. How can this boy feel potent? How can his sense of masculinity develop? How can his framework of manhood be shaped? How can he learn "The Man Rules"? And, most importantly, what self-attribution is he making about his own potency and masculinity that could be damaging his self-esteem and self-efficacy?

These youth who lack athletic prowess often feel rejected by their peers, especially in gym classes or other arenas in which athleticism or coordination is required. Fitzgibbons proposes, "This anguish can be so damaging to masculine identity that it can even override the psychological

---

103   Fitzgibbons, 2010

benefits of having a positive father relationship."[104] If a child is being ridiculed thusly, Fitzgibbons hypothesized that the resulting homosexual attractions and temptations will begin in approximately the sixth or seventh grade. He states, "The appeal is usually toward strong and athletic teenagers."[105] As it relates to gender role conflict, this may be the age at which jealousy of other males heightens. Typically, a child in the sixth or seventh grade is in the early stages of puberty where strong sexual feelings are emerging. If this is coupled with a desire for positive male attention, it is not surprising that some type of same-sex attraction may occur for males, whether the child is heterosexual or homosexual orientation.

Boys who experience a weak masculine identity are more likely to question their worth and value. The weak masculine identity and resulting poor self-image can lead to confusion on many levels of cognitive and emotional functioning.

Sexual Trauma in Childhood

Countless books and seminars have been devoted to the concept of sexual trauma in childhood. As a psychologist who primarily treats men in recovery or those who have experienced trauma, I hear daily of the effect sexual trauma has on men. Their stories can be absolutely gutwrenching, as sexual trauma can shake one's sense of self to the very core of their existence. The impact of the trauma may be immediate, delayed for years, or even lifelong.

When a man or older adolescent male sexually abuses a younger, developing child, it can have astounding effects on the psyche. If the abused

---

104   Fitzgibbons, 2010
105   Ibid

child is male, his masculinity undergoes an unthinkable assault. It is common for the child to blame himself for the abuse. Typical thoughts are, "I must be gay" or "the perpetrator must have seen something in me that told them they could do this to me." They immediately begin questioning their masculinity and often feel inferior to their male counterparts.

Countless times, I've heard my clients say something like: "I didn't stop them. I should have stopped them. Why didn't I stop them?" What has society's Man Rules engrained in the mind of these males about being able to defend themselves? These messages convey the belief that boys are meant to be strong and never weak; according to the Rules, we should be able to defend ourselves and fight off anything attacking us. To put it in casual vernacular, "If I am unable to fight for myself, I am a wimp. I am not strong, but a sorry excuse for a male. I am a wuss or a sissy."

Males often struggle with childhood sexual abuse, but especially if they enjoyed the physical sensation or were brought to orgasm. The feeling of enjoyment can cause them to deeply question their masculinity and sexuality. They think that if they derived pleasure from physical touch initiated by a member of the same sex, then they must be gay because no heterosexual boy would enjoy that feeling. They can also feel extreme anger at themselves for not stopping the abuse or for even returning to the abuser, knowing that it would happen again. Some victims are intensely angry with themselves, while others may even initiate a repeated abuse because of the intense sexual feelings they experienced. This is where the issues of Father Absence, Father Wound, and Father Hunger attempt to inappropriately resolve their dilemma. The victim's mind tells them, "No, this is inappropriate", but his body responds by sending the message, "Yes, this is pleasurable", and is fulfilling the male role they've so craved.

Some males are extremely angry with their body, feeling that it has betrayed them during the abuse. They question, "Why did my body respond? Why did I get an erection? Why did I have an orgasm? I didn't want this, so why didn't I stop it?" Naturally, these questions can lead to many feelings of gender role confusion and, at times, sexual identity confusion. When I discuss these concepts with sexual abuse survivors during therapy, the moments are very profound and emotive. Many of my clients have never disclosed their history to anyone, believing that no one could understand their feelings, their experience, and the ramifications they still face. But when another male can hear and empathize with their pain as I do, the hope of restoration begins.

Many of these victims are left feeling that their body betrayed them. It is amazing what a few lessons concerning sexual physiology, the reflex arc, and the sexual response cycle can do to aid in patients' understanding of why their bodies responded the way they did during an abusive situation. Our bodies respond to stimulation, whether it is wanted or unwanted, and are designed with certain reflexes to prepare us for incoming information and activity. When the body is stimulated with sexual information or activity, the sexual response cycle begins involuntarily. The body jumps into what is known as the excitement phase, during which various reflexes occur and chemical reactions activate. For example, upon the introduction of sexual stimuli, the male erection occurs. The complete sexual response cycle has four stages: excitement, plateau, orgasm, and resolution. In response to enough sexual stimuli, the body will carry out this cycle from beginning to end. This happens in situations of abuse *even when the sexual advance is unwanted*. Understanding why their body responded to such stimuli can often help to lessen the guilt and shame experienced by a victim of sexual abuse. Understanding these natural reactions can even assist with resolving the gender role conflict and sexuality confusion that can emerge as a result of sexual abuse.

It is often frustrating and confusing for the adult man who proclaims himself to be heterosexual to find that he desires, contemplates, or even returns to some type of same-sex behavior with another male. Some believe that this behavior manifests itself primarily in times of stress or depression. Often, the return to this behavior is a result of a trauma bond, where the victim is caught in a cycle of trauma repetition. In his book, *The Betrayal Bond*, Patrick Carnes, Ph.D. examines several trauma bonds that can develop in a person who has experienced similar sexual trauma. According to Carnes, some of these bonds entice the traumatized person to continue to repeat the trauma in various forms, including, but not limited to the following behaviors:

- constantly reliving the trauma mentally, emotionally, and/or physically;
- continuing to be drawn to the abuser;
- defending their abuser; or
- surrounding themselves with others who strongly resemble their abuser on a physical or emotional level.[106]

It is helpful to assist the victim in examining the ways they are experiencing a trauma bond. This can offer them a framework from which they can explain their confusing feelings and/or the behavior they cannot understand.

The pain and trauma of male sexual abuse can manifest in countless cognitive, emotional, spiritual, relational, gender, and sexual aberrations and distortions. Sexual identity confusion is only one of many symptoms a victim may or may not experience due to abuse. Frequently, when a person comes to therapy and works to discuss issues of a sexual nature (whether it be sexual identity confusion, sexual addiction, or sexual dys-

---

106   Carnes, 1997

function), the recommendation is often a trauma-based treatment program. The gender issues and confusion or sexual issues and confusion are frequently a byproduct of the original trauma. Males who are traumatized by sexual molestation typically experience some level of gender role conflict.

Excessive Responsibility

This concept can be coupled with ideas of enmeshment and emotional incest, especially in the relationship between a mother and son. If there is conflict or emotional distance in the parental marriage relationship, some mothers may be likely to foster inappropriate relationships with their children, particularly their sons. The mother may come to be dependent on the son to meet her emotional needs. She may share inappropriate details of the marital relationship, including her unhappiness, her concerns and discontent, and emotional neediness. Though it is not uncommon for sons to have a close relationship with their mothers, what are the implications when the boundaries of these relationships become blurred and unclear? When a young man feels an excessive or overwhelming burden of responsibility for his mother's emotions, it can have a tremendous impact on his development. The child will gauge his own behavior based on his mother's mood and perceived happiness. Often the child will thwart his own thoughts and desires in an effort to do what will satiate the need of his mother. Emotionally incestuous relationships, formed by unhealthy maternal bonds, as mentioned above, can result in diverse and destructive behaviors in the son such as rebellion, addiction, promiscuity, and sexual identity confusion. In the case of promiscuity, the son may be trying to conceptualize girls in a mental schema outside of the enmeshment he feels with his mother. In sexual confusion, he may want to escape the burden of the excessive responsibility he thinks will come with all females. In gender role conflict, he may have become overly identified with his mother and tends to emulate more feminine behavior.

Anger

Anger can lead to gender issues when the boy feels he cannot tolerate the anger he has toward himself and wishes to be the opposite gender or a gender variant. Additionally, his anger may take the form of strong jealousy towards other males who are perceived as the masculine ideal that he cannot achieve.

Additionally, there may be a sense of distress about their emotional state, which could lead to questions that ignite gender role conflict. In his article, Fitzgibbons proposed,

> The most significant type of anger influencing the development of homosexual attractions in childhood is anger with oneself. As a result of ongoing rejections by peers, many boys acquire an intense dislike for their bodies and view themselves as weak, unattractive, and un-masculine. They are so uncomfortable with their physiques that it is not unusual for them to spend a great deal of time fantasizing about escaping from their own bodies by assuming the body of another. This daydreaming can begin when they are young and may lead to a strong physical attraction for those of the same sex.[107]

This sense of anger toward the self can also result in gender role conflict. The male may feel that he cannot live up to the masculine ideal or to

---

107   Fitzgibbons, 2010

the males of whom he is jealous. He becomes angrier with himself for this inability to achieve ideal maleness and imagines himself to be more feminine, weak, and different than other males.

Pain of trauma

The purpose of this book is not to address, condemn, nor promote homosexuality or homosexual behavior, but rather to examine how the trauma experience can provoke psychological and emotional distress that can express itself in a variety of ways. It is imperative that all therapists carefully examine the role of trauma in the lives of their patients. The current trend for Cognitive-Behavior Therapies and Short-Term Solution Focused Therapies is concerning. I fear many therapists are causing more harm than good by not possessing the skill or knowledge base needed to properly examine the role of trauma in their patients' lives. Although Cognitive-Behavioral Therapy has value in these situations, it must be combined with other therapies that are designed to address trauma and deep psychological issues. Therapies such as Insight Oriented, Psychodynamic and Internal Family Systems are beneficial before engaging Cognitive-Behavioral Therapy. To my therapist readers, you cannot stay in the manifest content of what a person brings into session; you must listen astutely to the latent content and have the appropriate training and knowledge to understand human behavior and underlying psychological processes in order to provide effective treatment. For the victims reading this, please make sure any therapists you seek to work with have extensive trauma training and are willing to incorporate it into your healing process.

SELF-REFLECTION QUESTIONS

1. *How did you experience sadness and loneliness in your childhood? As an adult?*

2. *How did you experience fear and mistrust in your childhood? As an adult?*

3. *If male, did you have a weak or strong masculine identity as a child? How would you describe it today?*

4. *Have you experienced sexual trauma in your life? If so, have you worked through this with a trusted therapist?*

5. *Have you ever felt excessively responsible, emotionally or physically, for one or both of your parents?*

6. *Do you currently have anger toward yourself? If so, what is it and how is it manifested?*

7. *Have you suffered any other form of trauma?*

8. *Have you experienced the loss of a father or father-type figure?*

15

SPIRITUALITY, GENDER CONFLICT, AND SHAME

*"We are not human beings
having a spiritual experience ...
we are spiritual beings
having a human experience."*

— Unknown

Pia Melody writes, "Spirituality is the experience of being in a relationship with a power greater than self that provides acceptance, guidance, solace, serenity, grace or healing, love, and nondestructive creativity." [108] While I agree with her statement concerning spirituality, it has been my experience that people who claim to be spiritual can

---

often be judgmental and close-minded. Traditional Evangelical Christianity has distinct delineations between the genders. What is the impact of these delineations on men who are not like the Biblical examples of Samson, who had immeasurable strength; King Solomon, full of wisdom and lust; King David, a valiant warrior; Abraham, the father of many nations; or John the Baptist, a man of the wilderness? Consider the Biblical description of the brothers, Jacob and Esau, found in the book of Genesis. Jacob is described as a soft, smooth-skinned man who was close to his mother. Esau was described as a hairy, rough, and rugged hunter. The behaviors and descriptions of Esau, as well as the noteworthy men mentioned afore, depict strong, hyper-masculine ideologies of men, with the single exception of Jacob.

At times, the teachings of the Christian church may negatively impact a boy's sense of self. Some youth who struggle with gender role conflict may hear scriptures from the Bible that seem damning of someone like them and be left even more conflicted than before.

I Corinthians 6:9-10 says,

> Know ye not that the unrighteous shall not inherit the kingdom of God? Be not deceived: neither fornicators, nor idolaters, nor adulterers, nor effeminate, nor abusers of themselves with mankind, nor thieves, nor covetous, nor drunkards, nor extortioners, shall inherit the kingdom of God.[109]

A youth struggling with his gender identity might hear this passage, internalize the literal, superficial message and infer that the scriptures pertain directly to them. Some of these can lead to a faulty conclusion that God is not pleased with who they are. They can feel shamed, guilt-

---

109   The Bible, King James Version, I Corinthians, 6:9-10

ridden, and disconnected from their Higher Power because of how they interpret the scriptures.

Children and adolescents do not have the ability to interpret Biblical scripture in a scholarly, objective manner. Take for instance the verse from I Corinthians 6. Some Bible scholars have reported that the word "effeminate" in this scripture likely pertains to a man who has abandoned his sense of masculinity and accepted himself as a female. Given some interpretations, this scripture might only apply strictly to transgender individuals. Without context and definition, passages such as these continue to fuel the deep shame that brews within boys and may leave them with the foregone conclusion that God is displeased with them. Such seemingly fire-and-brimstone passages could easily invoke fear and shame in a religious youth who is struggling to understand his gender confusion.

However, the same Bible (KJV) contains passages like Psalm 139:14 "I will praise thee; for I am fearfully and wonderfully made; marvelous are they works; and that my soul knoweth right well." And Jeremiah 1:5, "Before I formed thee in the belly I knew thee; and before though cadets forth out of the womb I sanctified thee, and I ordained thee a prophet unto the nations." The Bible also tells us in Luke 12:7, "But even the very hairs on your head are all numbered. Fear not therefore: ye are of more value than many sparrows.[110] Such passages imply that God knows and loves each person for who and what they are, no matter the inner conflict. But if only the passage from I Corinthians 6 was read without a more affirming message like that found in Psalm 139 to accompany it, what kind of self-image would a young, gender-confused boy have of himself?

---

110   The Bible, King James Version, Psalms 139:4, Jeremiah 1:5, Luke 12:7

In Ben's situation, the religious environment in which he grew up contributed greatly to his struggle with social alienation. He was not allowed to attend his school's sporting events and was taught that organized sports were sinful, as those who participated placed their own worldly passions before their godly responsibilities. Confining concepts such as these can cause youth to view God as a judgmental, ominous entity and places unnecessary guilt, fear, and shame on these young people. As Ben matured, he realized that not all fundamental Christians believed such restraining, judgmental teachings as those to which he had been exposed. Such confinement attributed to religious principles can sometimes be referred to as spiritual abuse.

Spiritual abuse often comes in the form of an authority figure controlling others through the weapons of fear and condemnation. Spiritual abuse has the potential to be the origin of many cognitive distortions about God, the world, and personal relationships. Those who grow up in environments in which people in leadership roles have contributed to their trauma experiences often have an underlying feeling that authority figures do not care for them, regardless of how well they can function with these leaders. It can take very focused counseling to reframe these cognitive distortions and replace them with more accurate and objective thought processes. In Ben's case, his interpretation of religious teachings in self-damning ways further alienated him from his peer group and contributed to a rocky self-esteem and gender role conflict later in life.

Children and youth need encouragement from their spiritual leaders, not condemnation and rejection. They need to believe that God loves them and accepts them. There are many more scriptures about the love, grace, and acceptance offered by God than about condemnation and rejection. If a boy has "softer", effeminate traits or a girl has "dominant", masculine traits, God does not love or accept him or her any less. They are fearfully and wonderfully made.

SELF-REFLECTION QUESTIONS

1. *How do you define God?*

2. *What is your perception of how God sees you?*

3. *What role has spirituality, religion, and the Bible played in your beliefs about masculine and feminine roles of men and women?*

4. *What role has spirituality, religion, and the Bible played in your gender role development?*

5. *If you have experienced gender role conflict, has spirituality, religion, or the Bible played a role?*

6. *Have you experienced spiritual abuse?*

7. *What has been your positive or negative experience with clergy?*

16

AS THE CONFLICT DEEPENS

"Self-understanding rather than self-condemnation is the way to inner peace and mature conscience."

— Joshua L. Liebman

The years between ages 12 and 18 can be difficult for many adolescents. Many positive and negative events transpire during this time of development, which can impact one's sense of belonging and social acceptance. Adolescents attempt many new things while trying to decide what is right for them in life.

As a youth, Ben decided to try and play baseball and tennis. He attempted baseball while he was still in grade school. Unfortunately, baseball was a failure. No one bothered to stop and realize that he wasn't good because he didn't understand the game or the rules. As he reviewed his experience with the sport later on, he wondered if maybe they had explained the rules at some point and he had missed it, or they had simply assumed a boy in fourth grade would already know the rules of the game. Either way, baseball was not for him.

Tennis, on the other hand, went well. He and another girl won a trophy for being the best doubles team. Ben had finally found a sport. Did this mean he could now fit in with other boys and avoid being teased? Unfortunately, this was not the case at all.

After tennis matches or long periods of running, he would lie on the floor with excruciating pain in his legs, especially in his right knee. After a physical examination, the doctor recommended he be removed from most physical activity, including tennis and physical education class. The risk of breaking his leg was too high, and he had to be cautious until he was an adult and the bones had fully grown. Beginning in the sixth grade, he was removed from all physical activities. Ben sat in an extra study hall while the other students went to gym class. Boys tend to bond during physical education and with more physical contact activities, but he, once again, was on the outside.

Missing out on the locker room experience was both hurtful and helpful for Ben's development. He felt he could not compare physically to the alpha boys who were developing muscular bodies. As a boy, he failed to look around at the bodies of the typical average boy but rather focused on the emotional inferiority he felt towards the jocks. He did not feel masculine because of the gender role conflict he was experiencing: the lack of physical skills, the bullying, and now his body telling him he could not maneuver like a boy either. He didn't have the bone structure of other boys for physical endurance and sports. He worked at trying to fit into the male role of masculinity, but every time he made some strides ahead, something would go wrong and catapult him back to the other side. Why was this fight so difficult when it seemed so natural and easy for everyone else? Since Ben did not get to experience P.E., he never completely learned the rules of any sport. As a byproduct of being excluded from physical activity early in life, even now he struggles when conversing about sporting events, players, and specific plays due to a lack of knowledge.

When his fourth grade friend, Eric, moved away, Ben lost one of the only male friends he had. In middle school, however, he developed a new friendship with Jeff. He "learned a lot" at Jeff's house whose stepfather had *Playboy* magazines strewn throughout the house.

When he looked at the pictures of naked women in the magazines, his body started responding sexually. This only added to his confusion. Though he didn't like most things other males liked, he now identified with them and had similar responses and thoughts about girls. There was something about these pictures that caused him to want to be more than just friends with girls. Ben felt something much stronger — a drive, an impulse, a yearning. He started to see girls differently. It was like the desire he'd had in first grade to have his first girlfriend, but more animalistic and primal.

In his junior year of high school, the teasing decreased and people began to simply accept him as he was. However, the deep psychological damage had already been etched into his psyche. The layers of trauma had been compounding year after year, and no amount of acceptance in high school was going to heal the years of trauma he had already endured. The negative, self-deprecating loud speaker in his head had been blasting its hateful message for years, and he could hear little outside of its noise.

He became close friends with several girls in high school, secretly falling in love with them. He hoped that one day the girls would realize that they were not just friends, but were in love and would want the same level of relationship he desired. Sadly, this did not happen at this stage in his life.

At the end of high school, he was voted *"Most Changed."* He found this terribly ironic as he felt he had not changed at all; rather, some popular people had gotten to know him and realized that he was fun to be with. His award should have actually been *"Finally Accepted."*

Having only one date during high school, he sadly resolved that he would probably end up being asexual. By definition, an asexual person is someone who has no real interest in sex and lives in sexual solitude. Though he knew in his heart that he was not asexual (he had strong feelings of attraction and a healthy interest in sex), he didn't think he had much of a choice in the matter given his history and his misguided belief that girls only fell in love with alpha males.

Ben graduated from high school and moved on to college, where he made a close friend who was athletic. One night, during his roommate's basketball game, he was sitting in the bleachers with a group of girls who were talking about the players. Unexpectedly, the most beautiful girl in the group made a statement that shocked him to his core. She said, "You date guys like Mike, but you marry guys like Ben." He knew by the tone of her voice that she was not simply placating; she was serious and the other girls agreed with her. He sat silently, but the impact of that statement was deep. He began to believe that maybe girls could truly visualize him as a male counterpart, and being an alpha male was not as much of a requirement as he had once thought.

Ben went on with his college career and eventually graduated with several degrees over the course of 10 years. Eventually he found love and maintained a five-year romantic relationship with a woman named Lu. She was the one who finally allowed him to experience what it was like to be truly accepted by another person.

During this time, he also started personal therapy to deal with the trauma of his past. Throughout Ben's life, he could have been diagnosed with several disorders. There were times in which he clearly met the criteria for Major Depressive Disorder, Persisting Depressive Disorder, Generalized Anxiety Disorder, and Obsessive Compulsive Personality Disorder. Ben's therapist had no shortage of material to work with. This initial therapy was one of the greatest life-changing gifts that he received. It was the first place he openly discussed the pain he had experienced throughout his childhood. The psychologist started to help Ben make sense of his life experiences, worked to foster insight, and helped him feel like some of the hurt could maybe be resolved. Ben also began to build some degree of self-esteem and find ways to continue to move forward in his life. He found therapy to be exceptionally helpful. However, during the course of therapy, another life-changing event occurred.

Reconciliation

Between his junior and senior year of college, Ben returned home for a two-week visit and, sometime during his stay, his father requested to meet with him for lunch. However, he had no intention of meeting with that man. He was 21 years old and had never once been out to lunch alone with his father. He could only imagine the awkwardness and discomfort both he and his father would feel after the years of emotional disconnectedness.

The day before he returned to college, his mother told Ben that his father was angry with him for not acknowledging the simple request for a lunch. Ben's anxiety immediately started escalating. Though his father had provided for him financially, paying for everything from childhood toys to college tuition, no real relationship ever existed between them. Nevertheless, Ben acquiesced.

Meeting for lunch that day was pivotal. His father explained how frustrated he was that Ben had not wanted to meet with him, realizing how strongly Ben disliked him. Unfortunately, he was correct: Ben did not like his father and felt mostly contempt towards him. His father apologized for his lack of parenting, fathering, and involvement in his son's life.

Ben's father shared that he had lived through a childhood riddled with physical, verbal, and emotional abuse from his own father. Ben's father had been forced to start working from the time he could walk until he left home at 18. He had no great love for Ben's grandfather. He said that, as a child, he would yearn to be allowed time to play like other kids, being left alone from his father's demands. Ben's father made a vow to himself that he would not do this to his own children. Instead, he would leave his kids alone, let them be kids, and play — not control them as his father had.

Shocked at what Ben was hearing, his father's past behavior towards him began to make sense. He realized that his father did not hate him, nor did he ignore Ben out of cruelty or because of some sort of defectiveness on his part. Ben's father's responses toward him were out of love and, in his eyes, for Ben's safety. The father explained that he recognized how he had deeply hurt Ben, pushing him away from him. His father recognized he had caused as much damage as his own father had done to him, by going to the opposite extreme of parenting styles. He apologized for his actions and the impact it had on Ben's life. He asked if they could begin to have a relationship, and to be given a chance to get to know each other better from this point forward.

Ben remembers sitting in shock and amazement. He finally replied sincerely, "Dad, this is all I have ever wanted." Ben offered him forgiveness and agreed to build a relationship, even though neither of them had an example of a healthy father/son relationship to follow going forward.

This was a pivotal, memorable day in Ben's life. As he processed the conversation over and over on his own and in therapy, pieces of his life started to click. He had spent years telling himself that his father hated him — that he was so defective that his own father couldn't even muster the desire to love him. The resulting self-hatred and self-loathing was intense, deep, and cutting. Now, suddenly, he learns that his father did not feel this way, but was trying to protect him from the pain he had experienced in his own childhood. Ben finally knew that God, life, and his father were all trying to give him a gift of healing in their own way, and he accepted the gift with thankfulness. He continues to be grateful for that conversation and the years that have followed of building a new adult relationship with his father, whom he has grown to deeply love and appreciate.

A person's perception is their reality. The motivation and intentions of his father's heart was the exact opposite of what Ben had interpreted and experienced. Though miles now separate them, Ben has grown to love his father dearly and spends as much time with him as possible. Their early relationship may not have been perfect but their current bond is one of the greatest gifts Ben has ever received.

Ben's healing from toxic shame and trauma was a result of doing a great deal of emotional work, introspection, therapy, writing, and self-care. Even after the pivotal conversation with his father, it took many years to undo the harmful effects of years of toxic shame and trauma he experienced.

Ben's father determined to be different from his own father. In his mind, this was the way to be an appropriate father — one who did not abuse and misuse his own children. When individuals decide to do the exact opposite of their parents, it is often done out of a strong emotional reaction. In their mind, the only logical way to right the wrong that has been done to them is to do the polar opposite.

In *Facing Codependency*, Pia Melody describes the process specifically:

> When children see their caregivers being immoderate in matters of dress, in their attitude toward their bodies, in the way they think and solve problems, in the expression of their emotions, and in their behavior, they model their reactions after those of the caregiver. Some codependents who didn't like what Mom and Dad did do exactly the opposite, but because what they are reacting against is in the extreme, their 'solution,' the opposite behavior, is also in the extreme.[111]

While teaching psychology classes for the past 15 years, I often tell my students, "You can only take a client as far as you have gone." I think it is extremely important for therapists to do their own work, process their own journey, have insight into their own self, and experience the process of change in their own lives. A therapist needs to experience the same healing and change process that they guide clients through. Experience is often the best teacher. I believe therapy to be helpful to all individuals.

---

111   Melody, 1989

I often say, "There are only two kinds of people in the world: those who have a therapist, and those who need a therapist."

Emotional pain for men is real, and I believe, often under-addressed. There are many men who have been hurt by gender role conflict, toxic shame, and complex trauma. I have dedicated the majority of my career focusing on the treatment of men — those who have experienced bullying, sexual, and/or physical abuse, and those whose lives have been caught up in addictions while trying to numb the underlying, deep seated pain of trauma. Men, too, need a place to talk, a place to be heard, and a place to find healing.

Marriage

While Ben attended graduate school, he met and married a woman named Annalisa. Their lives have complemented each other in remarkable ways. She is familiar with his struggles: Ben is an adult male who knows little about male-driven tasks. His wife was raised in a more male-driven environment and is rather handy with home repairs. After being raised in a male-centric environment, his wife did not want to marry an alpha male. She had grown up in a house in which sports played on the television continuously. She was actually happy that Ben hated sports and had no desire to watch them. Ben and his wife have been married for numerous years and have children of their own.

SELF-REFLECTION QUESTIONS

1. *What was your experience, both positive and negative, being involved in sports?*

2. *Did you experience any physical problems that interfered with the process of development?*

3. *What was positive and negative concerning your locker room experience as a youth?*

4. *What was your experience of comparing yourself to others? What was your assessment? How did you measure up?*

5. *What roles do you think close friends or other peers made in your overall development?*

6. *What harmful messages were being played about yourself in your own head during adolescence?*

7. *As a youth, what did you fantasize your adult love relationships would be like?*

8. *If you have been involved in therapy, what has been your experience and how did it help you?*

9. *What has transpired in your adult life that has helped you now make sense of childhood events?*

17

RESULTS OF GENDER ROLE CONFLICT, SHAME AND COMPLEX TRAUMA

"Unexpressed emotions will never die.
They are buried alive and will come forth later
in uglier ways."

— Sigmund Freud

"Until you make the unconscious conscious,
it will direct your life, and you will call it fate."

— Carl Jung

Fortunately, throughout Ben's difficult life journey, he did not resort to the use of drugs or alcohol to numb his pain. He attributes this to the values his parents and church environment imparted to him from an early age. Alcohol was never kept in his home, nor did he ever see his parents use cigarettes, alcohol, or drugs. He admits that there were many times that he wanted to numb the pain in some way, but he never actually turned to a substance. He is thankful for the values instilled in him by his parents. There are some attributes and actions he recognized in his parents that he has carried with him and has tried to replicate with his own children.

For many who experience gender role conflict, toxic shame, and complex trauma, the outcome is not so fortunate. Many adolescents and adults cannot endure the pain buried deep within them and turn to self-injurious behaviors, alcohol, drugs, violence, and suicide. Pollack has conducted a great amount of research about boys and their views of themselves, reporting, "The great majority of [boys] associate the prospect of becoming a man with negative outcomes — being overworked, lonely, depressed, and/or unloved."[112]

Negative Consequences and Destructive Behaviors

Having been a psychologist for the past 20 years, I have heard countless stories of pain and anguish and have seen the terrible impact of detrimental behaviors in the lives of my patients. I have treated children as young as 11 that are addicted to pornography and alcohol. For some, the unbearable pain starts early and release is imminent. Many will walk in silence, screaming with torment inside. Many continue participating in harmful behaviors well into their adult years before finding a healthy way to relieve the misery.

Internal emotional pain has countless origins. I will only review a few areas in this chapter, but remember that almost any behavior, when

112   Pollack, 2006

overdone, can become a problem in a person's life. Toxic shame can be caused by anything that can attack the soul. Complex trauma can be compounded by immeasurable sources of behaviors, including gender role conflict. Though gender role conflict can be common to everyone to some degree, some adolescents experience this conflict on a deep, emotional level. When gender role conflict is coupled with the degradation of bullying by peers, psychological damage is almost inevitable. The degree of shame experienced by the individual becomes toxic and an attack is turned inward on the self. But how exactly does gender role conflict lead to unhealthy thoughts, belief systems, and behaviors?

Joseph Pleck proposed that one area of gender role strain is gender role dysfunction, the idea that gender role standard fulfillment can have negative consequences. He states that the behaviors and characteristics that these standards prescribe can be inherently dysfunctional and can result in negative outcomes for the male.[113] Earlier I discussed "Masculinity Ideology", an idea in which males who adhere to a stereotypical masculine set of ideologies have a greater tendency to persist in unhealthy behaviors and experience consequences that are dysfunctional for themselves and for others around them. For example, some men hold traditional beliefs about their role as a father and what their role is concerning childcare and housework in relation to masculinity. From two national samples, Pleck reported that fathers who spend less time performing housework and child care tasks report lower levels of well-being.[114]

The study of masculine ideology has continued for the last three decades and findings support the negative consequences, both psychologically and physically, concerning the traditional male gender role. In 1984, researchers from the University of Connecticut, Donald Mosher, Ph.D.

---

113   Pleck, 1995
114   Pleck, 1995

and Mark Sirkin, Ph.D. developed a Hyper-Masculinity Inventory that has been used to correlate hyper-masculinity with drug use, aggressiveness, driving after drinking, and delinquent behavior.[115] The scientific journal "Psychology of Men and Masculinity" has published many articles reporting that men experience many diverse problems when they adopt and stick to traditional masculine ideology. This journal is an excellent source of research concerning the male experience.

Many men feel a significant amount of pressure to maintain a masculine persona; however, trying to achieve an idealized sense of masculinity can be daunting. Clinical psychologist Paul Efthim, Ph.D. and Boston College professors Maureen Kenney Ph.D. and James Mahalik, Ph.D. wrote a journal article entitled "Gender Role Stress in Relation to Shame, Guilt and Externalization", which identified a significant amount of research indicating gender role stress in men is related to anger and hostility, social fears, Type A behavior, elevated blood pressure, and high-risk health habits such as smoking and alcohol consumption.[116] According to Robert Zeglin, Ph.D., who has studied portrayal of masculinity in movies, conformity to traditional masculine norms has been associated with increased emotional distress including loneliness, anxiety, depression, and neuroticism.[117]

If men are not living up to their masculine or hyper-masculine ideologies, shame is likely to emerge. As discussed in earlier chapters, shame is mostly a harmful emotion that tends to grow and fester, easily becoming toxic. Shame has many detrimental impacts on the human psyche. Research has shown a connection between shame and poor psychological

---

115   Mosher, Sirkin, 1984
116   Efthim, Kenney, Mahalik, 2001
117   Zeglin, 2016

outcomes, such as depression, irritability, anger, and externalization.[118,119] Research further confirming this connection was conducted by Richard Eisler, Ph.D with empirical studies finding an inverse (opposite) relationship between gender roles, stress, and measures of physical and psychological well-being for both men and women.[120]

Claudia Black writes,

> We feel our pain. We medicate our pain. We rationalize our pain. These are all responses to the pain we have felt for so long. We first respond to pain on an emotional level, most commonly in terms of victimization, rage, and depression. In an attempt to control the pain, we may respond with behaviors trying to medicate it such as alcohol, food and drug abuse, or compulsive behaviors related to sex, money, or relationships. Last, we may respond on a rational level, thinking we can avoid the pain if we don't do anything to cause it. Perfectionism and procrastination are two cognitive attempts to control pain by avoiding it.

As humans, we want to escape, or even avoid, pain if at all possible. The quest for avoidance can be rational or irrational; logical or illogical; active or passive; and full of emotion, or totally emotionless. Whatever the method, pain is inescapable. It will catch up to you in some form or fashion. The only way to effectively deal with pain is to face it and work through it.

In 1995, in a chapter of his book, *A New Psychology of Men*, psychologist Steven Krugman cites Lansky, writing,

---

118   Tangney, 1991
119   Tangney, Wagner, Fletcher, Gramzow, 1992
120   Eisler, 1995

Compulsive patterns of behavior, such as workaholics, over-commitment to exercise routines, gambling, or perverse sexuality, derive their considerable power from the effectiveness in minimizing and controlling shameful states of feeling, often by numbing and dissociating the painful affect. Domestic violence — particularly wife battering — is in large measure a shame-driven interpersonal pattern in which feelings of dependency, abandonment, anxiety, and humiliation threaten men with psychological disorganization.[121]

The high consumption of pornography is another area that has become significantly problematic for men in the last 30 years. It is so significant that I feel it necessary to discuss it in some detail. It is well known that access to pornography via the internet is as easy as the click of a button — the days of sneaking into an adult store to rent or purchase these items are now over. Pornography is a problematic epidemic in today's world. There are many software companies that work to filter out adult content in an effort to keep children safe and to assist adults who are attempting to refrain from the use of pornography. One such company is Covenant Eyes. Their website provides a wealth of statistics about the pornography industry, the use of pornography by various age groups and groups of people, and discusses the dangers of pornography. On the site, they report that 35 percent of teen boys say they have viewed porn videos "too many times to count." According to Covenant Eyes, the pornography industry is earning billions of dollars each year.[122]

Phillip Zimbardo Ph.D and Nikita Duncan conducted a survey as part of their e-book, *The Demise of Guys*, and found that 59 percent of teenage boys, aged 13 through 17, and 60 percent of men, aged 18 through 25,

---

121   Krugman, 1995
122   Gilkerson, 2013

said watching pornography relieved stress and believed it had positive psychological effects. Zimbardo and Duncan cite the work of Sonya Thompson from the University of Alberta, Canada, who reports that one in three boys is now considered a "heavy" porn user, with the average boy watching nearly two hours of porn every week.[123]

As a practicing, clinical psychologist who treats chemical and behavioral/process addictions, I believe the 35 percent of teenage boys who frequently view pornography, as reported by Covenant Eyes, is a rather conservative number. Teen males commonly admit to regularly viewing pornography. Some report using it only as an aid to masturbate, while others are addicted to the pornography itself. The youngest boy I have treated for pornography addiction was 11 years old. He would shake from withdrawal symptoms. Boys as young as 11 years old have also been seen for the same reason by other colleagues in my office. I dare to say this is an epidemic for this generation of males.

My major concern about this behavior is not only the chronic use of pornography, but the overall message it is sending to young boys and men about the role of masculinity and sexuality. The specifics of this issue were discussed earlier in Chapter 13. In counseling, I have met several late high school and college age young men who are afraid to date out of fear of becoming sexually active, believing they are physically and sexually inadequate. They have come to believe it is easier and quicker to use pornography and masturbation to sexually relieve themselves than it would be to invest in a true relationship, ultimately saving themselves the possibility of future loss and/or humiliation. The experience I see in therapy with young men fits the information presented by Dr. Phillip Zimbardo in his TED talks and e-book.

---

123   Zimbardo, 2012

Zimbardo writes,

> The takeaway message for porn viewing is likely to be ego-deflating because of the assumption that what you see is what is the norm, the acceptable way to perform, the appropriate way to relate to a sexual partner; worst of all, you see that size not only matters but dominates.[124]

Young men need to understand that what they see in pornography is not an accurate portrayal: the actors take breaks, get assistance with erections from vasodilation medications or injections, and use penis pumps or vacuums. But when a young teen is not aware of these tricks, the male identity of the teen suffers, and they can feel demoralized. Additionally, chronic pornography use can impact a male's sexual functioning and ability to achieve or maintain an erection

It does not take a scientist or a psychologist to understand the detrimental effects of porn on masculine ideology. What degree of shame must the chronic consumption of pornography engender in the minds of males? Again, the male feels that they cannot compare or "measure up" to their porn star male counterparts, creating a source of shame. If statistics are correct that adolescent males are watching up to two hours of pornography a week, that also translates to two hours of harmful attacks on the male's self-esteem. It is two hours of shame-inducing indulgence. It's a mix of pain and pleasure that is ultimately detrimental to their self-worth.

There are many problems men can experience by adhering to masculine ideologies and attempting to deaden their inner strife. Research has identified the male ideology as a culprit that shuns help-seeking

---

124   Zimbardo, 2012

behaviors in men and contributes to their unwillingness to seek counseling and psychotherapy.[125, 126] Males — faced with so many problems as a result of masculinity ideology, pornography, bullying, and trauma — can still be resistant to seeking help.

Many of the destructive behaviors that are employed, in an effort to numb internal pain, have a strong addictive quality to them and require some type of professional intervention for proper termination. This includes, but is not limited to, the use of alcohol and psychoactive substances, pornography, gaming, gambling, and violence. If an addictive behavior pattern emerges by the age of 14, it is likely to be a life-long struggle. The National Institute on Drug Abuse reports that if an adolescent is drinking by the age of 14, he or she is likely to have an alcohol abuse or dependence problem in their adulthood. If an addictive process begins at this young age and develops into a clinically defined addiction, the male now has co-morbidity, with the shame and trauma from the original hurt now coupled with an addiction driving their life in an uncontrollable cycle of pain and self-destruction. Visit any 12-step meeting and the room is full of individuals who once thought the chronic use of a substance was the only way to subdue their inner turmoil and quiet their shame.

Granted, addictive cycles are not the only way to numb or escape pain. Some men tend to isolate and struggle to form and maintain relationships with other men and may even avoid forming male friendships at all. Men may feel vulnerable or feel they may be setting themselves up for further rejection by a male. They may struggle with the belief that they will not be accepted by other men, either because of some mannerism or lack of knowledge about manly things. It is also difficult because

---

125   Mahalik, et al, 2003
126   Pederson, Vogel, 2007

many men want to participate in activities that are more physical, like sports or hunting. A male with gender role conflict may feel unsure of how to act with another man and may not be accustomed to the company of males. If there is something about a person's presentation that is more feminine in nature, a man with gender role conflict may struggle with the thought that others might conclude that the two are homosexual partners.

Emotional Consequences

Problematic emotional states, such as depression and degrees of anger ranging from irritability to rage, are another detrimental impact of gender role conflict, toxic shame, and complex trauma. Psychoanalytic theories have defined depression as anger turned inward, and it has been theorized that rage is a result of prolonged shame.[127] However, anger and rage appear to be socially acceptable emotions for males, while the sensitive emotions are seen as un-masculine. Covington, Griffin, and Dauer proposed the concept of the Anger Funnel, which is defined as men, when experiencing feelings of hurt, sadness, fear, and insecurity, converge these emotions into a funnel and expel them as anger, rage, or violence.[128] How many men have learned that it is only safe to express emotion in the form of anger? Anger is empowering: people are threatened by it; they leave you, the aggressor, alone; you are no longer bullied; and your anger serves as a guard to ward off the more sensitive emotions. Rage can be as addictive as substances. In fact, many of the same mental processes and chemical reactions occur in the limbic system when using a substance as they do when you give in to rage.

127 Lewis, 1995
128 Covington, Griffin, Dauer, 2013

According to the American Psychological Association, the National Institute of Mental Health (NIMH) estimates that approximately six million men struggle with depression each year, but they are far less likely to seek treatment than their female counterparts are. Also, "four times as many men as women die by suicide in the United States, which may result from a higher prevalence of untreated depression. Yet eight out of 10 cases of depression respond to treatment."[129] These statistics are unfortunate yet true. Men often do not recognize the signs of depression and are much more likely to experience depression symptoms as anger, irritability, and a lowered frustration tolerance than the stereotypical symptoms of sadness and hopelessness. Some may even resort to violence as a result of depression. Men, often not experiencing full ranges of emotion, may not register the feeling of sadness that would be expected from most people suffering from depression. Men may become more reckless and compulsive in their interests, hobbies and other unhealthy behaviors, such as drugs and/or alcohol, to numb their emotions or to quiet the anger. Many men drown their depression in alcohol or mask it via drug use and may not even recognize depression as the underlying culprit of their problematic use of mood-altering substances. Additionally, it is more acceptable for a man to complain of physical symptoms such as headaches, muscle stiffness and pain, stomach ailments, and sexual difficulties than to identify depression as an emotional state. If you are a man, or a woman with a man in your life that you care about, be aware that depression often manifests itself differently in men than in women. The medical books can describe depression and develop criteria for diagnostic purposes, however, further research and my own clinical experience has shown that men and women have different expressions of depression.

---

129   American Psychological Association, 2005

Of paramount concern is the rising number of male suicides. Research reports males are under-performing scholastically compared to females, have significant issues with self-esteem, and the rates of depression and suicide in boys is growing rapidly.[130,131,132] The American Foundation for Suicide Prevention (AFSP) reports that there are 3.6 male suicides for every female suicide, but twice as many females as males attempt suicide.[133] This is simply because males often chose a more decided method, such as a gunshot wound. Of the suicides in 2016, the AFSP reports that 50 percent were committed through the use of firearms.[134] The World Health Organization (WHO) reports that, in the last 45 years, suicide rates in general have increased by 60 percent.[135] The National Institute of Mental Health recently updated the statistics on suicide with the latest trends from the Center of Disease Control and reported that:

- Suicide is the 10th overall leading cause of death in the U.S.

- Suicide is the second leading cause of death among people aged 10-34, and the fourth leading cause of death for those aged 35-54.

- In 2016, male suicide rates were four times higher (21.3 per 100,000 males) than for females (6.0 per 100,000 females).

- The highest rate of suicide among males was for those 65 and older (32.3 per 100,000 males).[136]

130   Pollack, 1998
131   Pollack, 1999
132   Poe, 2004
133   American Foundation for Suicide Prevention, 2016
134   American Foundation for Suicide Prevention, 2018
135   World Health Organization, 2018
136   National Institute of Mental Health, 2018

Some of the top reasons for suicide have been identified as: unemployment, loss of a loved one, sexual orientation, difficulties developing one's own identity, and rejection by one's own community or social/belief group. The horrific suicide rates as a result of bullying were discussed in Chapter 8.

No matter the source, gender role conflict, toxic shame, complex trauma, and a host of other problems are destroying the lives of men on a global scale. More research needs to be conducted and more dollars need to be spent to reach out to men who are suffering and help wipe away the stigma that surrounds men seeking psychological treatment for their problems. As a member of the mental health community, I want to raise awareness regarding the needs of men and help them get the help they need.

SELF-REFLECTION QUESTIONS

1. *What unhealthy behaviors are present in your life as a result of Gender Role Conflict?*

2. *What unhealthy behaviors are present in your life* outside *of Gender Role Conflict?*

3. *Has Gender Role Conflict and shame lead to trauma or a complex trauma?*

4. *Do you struggle with a chemical or behavioral addiction?*

5. *Do you struggle with depression, anxiety, or some other mental health problem?*

6. *Do you have a problematic relationship with pornography?*

7. *What negative impact has pornography had on your beliefs about yourself?*

8. *What negative impact has pornography had on your views of women?*

9. *Has pornography made you feel inadequate or inferior as a man?*

10. *Has pornography impacted your sexuality?*

11. *Are you resistant to getting help with your issues? If so, why?*

18 | 25 TIPS

"*Parents can only give good advice or
put them on the right path, but the
final forming of a person's character
lies in their own hands.*"

— Anne Frank

This book would not be complete without providing a road map to help parents and parental figures raise children in a healthy way, or without offering help to boys and men to overcome their gender role conflict, toxic shame, and complex traumas. In this next chapter, I will offer 25 tips for parental figures. It has been established that parenting is an extremely difficult but rewarding task that comes with many challenges. No parent will be perfect, but it is important that you are a "good enough" parent. A "good enough" parent is defined as one that does not strive to be perfect and does not expect their children to be perfect either. A parent will spend a lifetime attempting to implement the 25 tips provided in an attempt to be good enough and raise a well-functioning child.

1. Be a conscientious parent/parental figure and keep in mind the individual child's nature and unique personality. Keep Chapter 1 in mind and consider the five areas proposed by Pia Melody. How can you best communicate to your children that they are Valuable, Vulnerable, Imperfect, Dependent, and Spontaneous? Parental figures, whether they be biological parents, stepparents, adoptive parents, or foster parents, have a great responsibility for the well-being of their children; they are responsible for supplying the nutrients for the child's cognitive, social, spiritual, emotional, and physical growth and development.

2. Be a good listener: not only with your ears, but also with a 'third ear', hearing what is being said between the lines, even when not overtly spoken. Often, the issue the child brings to you is not the primary issue, but merely a symptom of the true, underlying issue. Asking questions, without being defensive or presumptuous, encourages them to better communicate and articulate their concerns. Be cognizant and aware!

3. Be a good examiner and investigator. Think about how things, events, and people in the child's life might impact him or her. Carefully critique what is allowed in your children's lives. Engage a supportive network of people who can mentor their strengths and refine their weaknesses. This is especially important if your child's interests differ from your own. My son takes after his mother's side of the family who like to hunt, fish, and engage in outdoor activities. Because these are

not areas of interests for me, I have worked to connect him with trusted men who can help him develop these skills.

4. Set an example of how to fully accept yourself as God/ Higher Power created you: an imperfect, emotional, flawed, unique human being. Children model both what they see and hear. If you disparage yourself, your children may follow this example and disparage themselves. But if you model a person who can tolerate and accept yourself for who you were created to be, your child has a better chance to develop a realistic, healthy self-esteem and spirituality.

5. Learn to laugh at yourself! Teach children to laugh at themselves and their mistakes. There is so much pressure in our society to be perfect, to look a certain way or get a certain score, that we no longer allow ourselves to make mistakes. Unrelenting standards can be a significant source of toxic shame. Help them learn that mistakes are to be expected and are no big deal.

6. Discuss The Boy Code or Man Rules with your son(s). What Man Rules are they aware of at different stages in their lives? What rules are they believing and applying to themselves? Where do they think The Man Rules are coming from? What Man Rules would they want to reject? What Man Rules do they feel are unfair and why? It's also important to discuss The Man Rules with your daughter(s), as well. This will help them understand both their unconscious and conscious expectations of males. It is important for females to identify their expectations of men to help them understand what type of male they are attracted to. Also of vital importance is the fact these daughters may, in the future, be mothers to one or more

sons. An understanding of The Man Rules is an important factor in the careful and thoughtful raising of children.

7. Discuss society's underlying messages to women with your daughters. What are the conscious and unconscious messages society sends to them? What are the expected codes of conduct for girls? How do Hollywood, social media, magazines, and enhanced/altered photos impact a girl's self-esteem? Find healthy ways for your daughter to build her self-esteem at all stages of development. Talk, also, to your sons about the roles of females, the challenges they face due to society's expectations, and the ways females may experience gender role conflict and gender restrictions.

8. Help your son(s) develop a definition of masculinity and your daughter(s) develop a healthy definition of femininity that is broad and inclusive. Help them understand that they do not have to fit a specific mold. Help them explore their own likes and dislikes, wants, wishes, and needs. Allow them to develop into the person that they are and were created to be. Help your son to know that he does not have to be a sports fanatic or player to be a true male, but can develop a number of diverse areas of interest. Explain interests have nothing to do with gender. In addition, your daughter does not have to keep up with the Kardashians in fashion, makeup, possessions, or looks, nor does she need to look like a supermodel. She, too, can develop her individual interests regardless of gender stereotypes.

9. Talk to your children about gender role conflict. Where do they feel different from children of the same gender? What

are their cross-gender likes? Do they label certain behaviors or interests as masculine or feminine?

10. Teach your child that vulnerability isn't a weakness. We are not born with innate knowledge and skills. Children learn by experimentation, guidance, and having a willingness to try new things. Help them understand and accept that they will not be good at everything, but encourage them to take healthy risks and try something new.

11. Educate your children about sex and sexuality. If you start teaching them at a young age about types of touch, privacy, and guidelines regarding physical and sexual engagement, open communication will be natural and less embarrassing for them as adolescents, when more significant questioning and teaching is necessary. I started teaching my children at a young age about their bodies, who could touch them, and how their genitals were only to be touched by themselves or a doctor when a parent is present. Throughout their childhood, I engaged with my children in age-appropriate conversation about the sexual abuse of children. I also reviewed appropriate and inappropriate touch when they would spend the night with friends or attend camps, etc. Additionally, I was open in teaching them that if someone attempted to touch them in a way that felt uncomfortable, they were to immediately tell their parents. I attempted to encourage them to trust their gut-reactions about people and touch, and to never be afraid of sharing their experiences with me. It was important to make sure that they knew that I would always support them. In early adolescence, we discussed issues of masturbation and sexuality in an open way. In a more stereotypical

fashion, I spoke with my son, and my wife spoke with my daughter. Even though my clients seem to be surprised I can think like a woman and tell them how their spouse is likely to respond, I am still male and do not have the experience of being female or having a female body. During discussions of sexuality, I approached these conversations in a straightforward, matter-of-fact way, and I encourage you do the same.

12. Notice when children are denying or aren't experiencing their feelings in a healthy way. Encourage them to stay present with their emotions and not be afraid of what they feel. Teach them that emotions are normal and healthy and serve an important purpose. Emotions are not right or wrong — they just *are*. It is what we do with emotions and how they are translated into behaviors that can be defined as right or wrong. Emotions are part of the human experience and are not to be avoided.

13. Encourage children to communicate. Help them learn to express themselves verbally and nonverbally. This may be exceptionally challenging with boys at various stages of development, especially in adolescence. Create a safe place for children to talk about their thoughts, feelings, behaviors, expectations, desires, and hurts.

14. Be vigilant regarding bullying, and be ready and willing to intervene, whether your child is being bullied or acting as the bully. Victims of bullying often become the bully in an attempt to regain the sense of power they've lost. If you find your child has been, or is being a bully, this may be a clue that they have been bullied. This is a prime example of my point above, about how a behavior may only be a symptom of a

deeper, underlying problem. As a parent, you have to resist the urge to overreact, and instead, have a heartfelt discussion with your child about their behavior and feelings. Children may not have the emotional capacity to make the connection that their aggressive behavior is in response to feeling powerless. Through open communication, you can help them understand the connection and address the root of the problem. This will also help them learn the important process of self-examination on a deeper level. Bullying is a critical time for intervention, and it is your responsibility to protect your children. If you see bullying in person, on social media, or in some other form, address it. Discuss the impact of the bullying. Don't ignore it or write it off as "kids being kids".

15. Look beyond the feelings or expression of anger to the underlying emotion. Children, and especially boys, will display anger as a primary emotion (remember the Anger Funnel). To be an effective parent, you need to look beyond the anger and examine the underlying emotions that may be outwardly manifesting as anger. Is the child in emotional pain, frustrated, embarrassed, or even tired? Look at all possible emotions, and don't examine only the surface.

16. Avoid being a "helicopter parent", rescuing your child from experiencing the natural consequences of life and their behavior. Life isn't fair and does not always work out the way we plan; it's important for children to learn this early on. I have trained my kids to understand that there are only a few types of 'fair' in life: the state fair, the county fair, the bus fare, and so on, but life is not on this list. Life has disappointments, and we make mistakes at times. Help them learn how

to accept defeat, disappointment, and consequences. Part of protecting a child is helping them learn what they are and are not responsible for.

17. Be connected to your children. Build a relationship with them. Treat them as individuals and recognize their thoughts, feelings, and values. Find out what is important to them. Converse with them about their opinions. Get to know them as people, rather than just as your children.

18. Recognize that respect goes both ways. As parents, we often demand respect from our children but don't give them respect in turn. It is our job to model mutual respect. They deserve to be respected and have their opinions heard and validated.

19. Educate them to the best of your ability about the opposite sex. What do they notice about the opposite sex? What do they like and dislike about the opposite sex? What characteristics do they see the opposite sex possessing? Which of those characteristics do they envy? Explain to them that the examination of their thoughts, feelings, and beliefs about the opposite sex will have an impact on their dating decisions and how dating behaviors develop. What are their biases about the opposite sex, and how do they consciously and unconsciously portray those in their beliefs and treatment of a dating partner? Help them examine how their childhood experiences and beliefs about the opposite sex will have an impact on how they interact with a dating partner in their adult life. For more help on this, I recommend you read the book, *For Men Only, For Women Only, For Young Men Only, For Young Women Only* by Shaunti Feldhahn. These easy-to-read books are based on sound research and large public polls.

20. Help them develop their own life goals. Do not try to fit them into your box or your idea of what you want them to be. Let them naturally develop by providing them many opportunities, and encourage them to explore. Sometimes, even what they excel at is not what they are most passionate about. For example, in school I was exceptional at biology and my father encouraged me to go into medicine. Even though I had an affinity for anatomy and physiology, my real passion was in psychology. My love for psychology was so strong that I often say that psychology chose me. Ultimately, my father encouraged me to pursue my own passion, not just the areas at which I excelled.

21. As a parent, don't let your own unresolved past negatively impact your child. Sometimes, parents try to resolve their own issues by living vicariously through their children. Examine yourself, resolve your own issues, and find your own healing. Throughout the book, there were numerous examples of parents who had unrealistic standards and expected outcomes for their children that were birthed out of their own hurts and traumas. Healing comes from doing your own work. Your child is a separate individual — allow them to be their own person.

22. Expose them to as many opportunities as possible. Let them be spontaneous! Let them try on many different hats until they find the one that fits them. Remember, our experiences shape us. Provide them with activities congruent with their abilities and desires.

23. Help them understand that while independence is a positive goal, they should expect that they will always experience

some degree of healthy dependence on others. We depend on others for some degree of love, support, friendship, comfort, and connection. No man is an island; we are relational creatures made to live in community with each other. The key is to find a healthy balance between independence and healthy dependence. Help a child understand that it is unhealthy to expect another person to complete them or to make them whole emotionally.

24. Help children learn the difference between passivity, assertiveness, and aggressiveness. Model how to use each of these skills appropriately in various situations. Not everything in life requires action. Help them learn to pick their battles.

25. Tell children often that you love them: text them; call them; tell them morning, noon and night; tell them after giving them praise; tell them after punishments. You can never tell them too often how much you love them!

SELF-REFLECTION QUESTIONS

1. *Which tips do you agree with?*

2. *Which tips do you disagree with?*

3. *What tips do you feel you are successfully implementing?*

4. *What tips do you feel need more work?*

FINDING HOPE, CLARITY, HEALING AND CHANGE

"We change our behavior when the pain of staying the same becomes greater than the pain of changing. Consequences give us the pain that motivates us to change."

— Henry Cloud

Hope

The process of healing from pain, loss, trauma, hurt, and disappointment is an arduous endeavor. Healing starts when one recognizes and admits that hurt and trauma have occurred and shame is present. Shame starts deep inside as a root and grows, outwardly affecting behaviors, relationships, and one's general approach to life. Some attempt to bury these issues, believing that, if buried deep enough, the problems would not germinate and be visible. For others, the shame comes out forcefully through rage, arrogance, and overbearingness. Still, some will become passive-aggressive, converting a response to the world in a co-dependent manner by working hard to meet the needs of others while simultaneously denying their own reality. Whatever method of behavior, the shame of past experiences lies deep within and will inevitably display itself through some form or other. There is no need to deny it: recognizing underlying hurt and shame is the first step in the journey of healing.

Let's take the Alcoholics Anonymous (A.A.) 12 Steps as an example. The first step states, "We admit we were powerless over our addiction — that our lives had become unmanageable." A.A. began in Akron, Ohio in 1935 and the 12 steps were published in 1939. For over 75 years, A.A. has helped people recover from alcohol addiction.[137] Why are they so successful? I believe the 12 steps are incredibly effective because they have the steps in the right order with 'identifying and admitting' as the first step.

The media frequently jokes about the 12 steps. Shows on television will often depict a middle-aged male entering a group of people and introducing himself, stating, "Hi I'm Ed, and I'm an alcoholic." However, this proclamation is no laughing matter. Admitting that there is a problem with your behavior is the most necessary first step. If we cannot admit to ourselves that shame resides within us, where can we begin the healing process? A.A. has been a source of hope, clarity, healing, and change for hundreds of thousands of people. Admitting you have a problem and need help to resolve it is the first step of finding hope. You are not alone and can find your road to your own recovery as well.

---

137   "Alcoholics Anonymous (AA), the 12-Step Program for Alcoholism Recovery", n.d.

Acknowledging the root of your emotional pain, loss, trauma, hurt, shame, or disappointment may not be an easy process. Anton, 29 years old, sat in my office for therapy after recently leaving a relationship with his verbally and physically abusive wife. Anton had scars from the physical abuse that had required medical attention and stitches. Throughout the session, he would recount stories of the abuse he had endured with a smile on his face, sometimes even laughing about it. I noticed this unusual behavior quickly, realizing that Anton was clearly not identifying with the pain he was experiencing. As time progressed, I learned that Anton's father died when he was only nine. Anton had personally seen his father crushed in a horrific bulldozing accident, adding great intensity to his loss. His mother had become depressed after her husband's loss, as she was left to raise several children on her own, with Anton being the youngest. Anton committed to being as helpful as possible to his mother and never be a burden. Somewhere, within his child mind, he came to the decision to keep a smile on his face and be the happy child that did not give his depressed mother anything else to worry about. All the while, Anton was living a lie, denying his own emotions and stuffing them further and further into the core of his existence.

Through the course of therapy, I gently confronted Anton about the incongruent nature between his words and the emotions that such a story would typically evoke with the current emotions displayed on his face and through his body language. I often pointed out to him that he was smiling or giggling. The first few times, he acted surprised that I, as the therapist, was having a reaction to his presentation. When he recounted these stories, I told him I was hurt for the little boy and the grown man who was carrying so much pain but wouldn't allow himself to experience it. After a few months of using the same intervention over and over, Anton started to identify with his own pain that had started on that dreadful day when his life forever changed before his eyes. He had to peel back layers of self-protection and self-preservation to find his true emotional self. The process towards admitting his deep pain took many therapy sessions and much modeling to let him know it was okay for a "manly man" to fully experience his emotions and begin the healing process. I knew, when the emotional wall of self-preservation finally collapsed, there would be a great deal of emotional trauma for Anton to work through. Until that time arrived, Anton could not be helped through the stages of experiencing and facing his trauma.

Not all cases are as difficult as Anton's, though. Many people are fully aware of their pain, hurt, trauma, and disappointment. It is the energy source driving their shame, depression, anxiety, addiction, or other unhealthy behavior. They recognize it fully for what it is and can readily admit to its existence. They can talk about it intellectually and/or emotionally. If you can acknowledge your pain, shame, or emotional state, you have taken the first step to finding healing and believing there is hope.

Clarity

How do you make sense of the trauma you have endured and the resulting shame you feel? Once a person acknowledges the trauma and shame, the next step is to find clarity. Clarity is the process of being able to look at your situation objectively while also identifying your subjective experience. You have always lived your life from a subjective point of view — noticing how you personally experienced it, how you felt, and the shame that took place within you as a result. Your perception is your reality. The way you experience something shapes your thoughts, feelings, and beliefs about the event, yourself, and your environment. Your perception becomes your truth. Clarification comes from recognizing that there is another reality besides the one in which you personally live. The reality of the situation may be different from your perception of it.

Such was the case in Ben's situation. He always assumed that his father didn't like him and wanted nothing to do with him, but as he later discovered, his father's avoidance of interaction was his way of protecting him and allowing Ben to be a kid, free from child labor and abuse. Once Ben received clarification regarding the facts of the event, he was able to see the situation more objectively and begin processing it on a level not available to him prior to this understanding.

Sometimes clarity comes from unexpected situations. Ben was not expecting to receive the information about his father's past on the day he finally shared his story. He was not expecting to find out that his father actually loved him and had been protecting him all along. Sometimes, circumstances and events will change your understanding of your trauma, but the shame can often persist. The death of a person, the unveiling of a secret, or the confession of another can alter your subjective perception. Objective knowledge is powerful.

Other times, there will be no life circumstances to provide clarity. You may simply know you do not like the way you feel, do not like yourself, and do not like the unhealthy patterns you continue to repeat. Clarity may have to come through professional intervention. It often takes processing life experiences with a trained professional to see there is another reality beyond the one you are living. Sometimes, having another person listen to your story and help navigate through the memories and emotions is the only way to find clarity. Over time, the waters of your thoughts have become so muddied with your experiences, shame, self-loathing, and pain that you cannot see clearly or objectively. Your future path may appear impassible, without a clear direction for making forward progress.

How do you find someone to help discover clarity? Locating a trusted and competent therapist can sometimes be a difficult process. You can find a long list of therapists in the phone book or online, but that does not mean that they are quality therapists with a background in trauma recovery. It is important to do adequate research before selecting a therapist. Ask questions about a prospective therapist's specializations to help you make an informed decision about which therapist is a good fit for you.

The therapeutic relationship established between a therapist and a client is of paramount importance. Many counseling textbooks will cite research stating that it is not necessarily the type of therapy that facilitates healing, but the strength of the therapist/patient relationship. Finding a therapist you connect with and trust, is a must. You are going to share your most intimate secrets and your innermost thoughts and emotions with this person. You must be able to establish trust with this individual and feel safe and unconditionally accepted. If these relational aspects are not present, most individuals will not remain in therapy and will fail to reach full healing. If you are in a therapeutic relationship lacking in trust and safety, or do not feel it is productive — move on! Find someone who provides you with a sense of internal peace, trust, and safety.

Even though the therapeutic relationship is the foundation of successful treatment, I do think the therapist needs to have the explicit specializations you might desire. Look for a therapist who has experience and knows a variety of techniques for treating trauma. Though this is not an inclusive list, ask if your therapist is versed in EMDR (Eye Movement Desensitization Reprocessing); somatic experiencing and body work by Peter Levine, as described in his book, *Waking the Tiger*; and/or the work of Dr. Bessel van der Kolk and his many suggestions in his latest book, *The Body Keeps the Score*. These are some modalities that can help a trauma patient.

Additionally, there are many different types of therapies in the field of psychology and counseling. Most insurance companies try to mandate the use of Cognitive-Behavioral Therapy (CBT), which is usually a fairly quick, short-term therapy. Naturally, insurance companies see it as cost-effective. However, this does not mean that it is patient-effective. The premise of CBT is that one's cognitive distortions and/or irrational thoughts are causing situational interpretations, which lead to false beliefs, and thereby, result in misdirected behavioral responses. Although there is accuracy to these assumptions, I believe CBT is only effective to treat certain cases or only effective to a degree, like for treating fears and phobias. It can be useful to examine the faulty beliefs and cognitions about oneself or the preconceived notions of gender and gender roles. However, if CBT is used with a trauma patient, I do not believe it should be the primary method of therapy used; it is best if coupled with other, more effective, forms of therapy. A person experiencing trauma and shame has deeper issues to resolve beyond cognitive distortions. I encourage individuals to search for therapists, trained in the areas of Psychodynamic theory, Internal Family Systems, and other Interpersonal type therapies. Therapists who are familiar with these modalities, combined with an understanding of trauma neurobiology, should be effective in treating the trauma patient. Finding a qualified therapist may take some effort. Do research and interview therapists with these considerations in mind. It is your right as a consumer to locate the appropriate person for your needs.

New patients frequently tell me that they have no interest in delving into their past but want only to resolve their current problem. I always interpret this one of two ways: either the patient is not fully educated about the purpose of therapy, or the patient is not yet ready for the rigorous process of effective therapy work. Though there are those who need help working through a current, specific problem, most people are truly an amalgamation of their experiences. Experiences shape us and become our reality, guiding our present behavior. How can you solve a present problem without fully examining how your current belief system was formed? If the current problem you are experiencing is a repeated pattern, this indicates that deeper work needs to be done. An examination of your past will most likely be helpful in uncovering important information and promote healthy change.

Freud and other early psychoanalytic theorists may have taken more of a parental-blame approach. However, effective therapy is not about finding or placing blame, whether it is from past experiences with parents or other prominent figures in one's life. Therapy is a journey of walking through your experiences to glean understanding from your past life events. It is concerned with looking at the subjective and becoming objective; it helps you examine the factual. Remember the five areas of healthy development of a child as proposed by Pia Melody: Value, Vulnerable, Imperfect, Dependent, and Spontaneous. Therapy examines the experience of each of these concepts. Trauma may have occurred not because of events, but perhaps what wasn't included as part of the developmental phase. For example, Ben's father's lack of involvement in each of these areas had a profound effect on Ben's gender role conflict and gender identity development. Therapy is often an examination of where your development may have gone awry due to abuse, neglect, specific traumas, and the experience of shame. It is typically about the process, not the "who" that caused changes to a belief system. Often, significant life players will be discussed, and there can be specific individuals at the source of pain and trauma, but healing does not come through the placement of blame. Healing comes through objective clarity — releasing the binding shame and resolving the necessary steps through the interventions of therapy.

Many therapists will ask new clients what their goals are for therapy. This may be the therapist's attempt to identify expectations, receive insight into a client's issues, and determine where they may already be within the stages of healing. Before entering therapy, it is helpful, though not necessary, for patients to consider their expectations and how these translate into personal goals. Though helpful, clients often cannot express specific goals, but only problem identification: they can communicate the problem and identify a behavioral pattern they want to change. Finding clarity about what you need from counseling may be part of your therapy process. It is not a requirement to enter treatment with goals in place.

Healing

The healing stage of therapy, or what is also known as the "working through" stage of therapy, is where the real work takes place. By the time a patient reaches this point, they should have established a trusting, caring therapeutic relationship. It is now time to delve into the individual's story. In the healing process, the therapist leads the patient in fact-examination and feeling-identification; helps the patient construct a coherent whole from these pieces allowing objective insight; aids in challenging their thoughts and subjectivity; and helps the client determine what is worth keeping and what can be discarded.

For many, the underlying trauma and shame has remained a secret. It is a force lying deep within and is often well defended. Many people have worked for years to keep these parts from ever being seen by another human being; only the pillow on their bed is aware of the tears and the pain they have endured. As I mentioned earlier, "You are only as sick as your secrets." Our secrets grow within us, often increasingly distorting our reality. For many who begin therapy, they initially cannot fathom telling another person their subjective experience.

The process of finding your voice and sharing the inner self can be gut-wrenching, but in the long run, it can be extremely rewarding Clarence, who is now in the later stages of his life, has become depressed. His family noticed he was increasingly lethargic and unmotivated. They did not understand why Clarence was depressed and encouraged him to seek out a counselor. Upon my early sessions with Clarence, it was clear that he is in the stage of Generativity vs. Stagnation, according to the psychosocial developmental stages proposed by Erik Erickson. In this stage, individuals face the internal decision of finishing out their life with vigor and energy by making the most out of retirement and their "golden years", or deciding to crawl into their proverbial recliner or rocker, and wait for time to pass until the end of their life. Part of the process of this stage is an examination of one's life, replaying and rethinking the events of the past and what their life has meant. Unfortunately for Clarence, his past holds many secrets that are damaging to his emotional well-being.

As an adolescent, Clarence was molested by another adolescent. Before this, he had been sheltered, with no exposure to information or experience of a sexual nature. Clarence was introduced to sex by another male teen friend and came to enjoy the sexual release he experienced during their activities. Eventually, his adolescent friend moved away, which no longer provided the opportunity for these sexual encounters. Clarence decided, in his late teens, that he would sexually educate younger boys and sexually molested several younger males. He exposed 7-, 8-, and 9-year-old children to pornography and various sexual acts. He reports, at the onset of this behavior, he did not realize he was sexually molesting these children, only thinking he was, "doing them a favor by showing them the ropes."

Fifty-five years later, Clarence realizes the gravity of his past actions and the trauma he must have caused the young boys. Riddled with guilt and shame as he struggled to accept what he had done, Clarence slipped into major depression. In our sessions, he continually states that there was no sex education provided in his youth: no public or private discussion of sexual molestation and inappropriate sexual touch. When his adolescent friend introduced sexual activity to Clarence, he thought this is what boys do together until they are old enough to find a wife. He embraced this false assumption and faulty experience, recreating it with others. Throughout our sessions, Clarence repeatedly says he planned to carry these secrets to his grave. He admits that, as he moved into his adult years and the topic of sexual molestation became more of a public issue, he realized the nature of his indiscretions. He could not fathom telling another person his deepest secrets. However, as therapy progressed, he started seeing the value of releasing his secrets, beginning to work through his own trauma and his past actions.

Finding the courage to tell your story and to expose your secrets to another person is powerful. It may be hard in the beginning, but secrets lead to isolation and shame that tend to bind oneself. You deserve to be free — you deserve to heal. Believing that you deserve to heal is another essential step toward that healing. A therapy room is not a courtroom and judgment has no place there. Rather, therapy is about finding a safe place to share your story. As a therapist, my role is to help people feel comfortable enough to tell their story, allowing them to finally release their secrets and destroy their shame.

In *A Man's Way Through Relationships*, sociologist Dan Griffin writes,

> If shame is the belief that there is something inherently and fundamentally wrong with you, the way you heal from all of the ways that corrosive thread has woven itself around your life is by taking the risk of facing those lies and sharing them with others. We allow ourselves to be seen — emotionally and spiritually naked — and we survive it, little by little we erase shame from our lives. That comes through the process of vulnerability.[138]

Through vulnerability, one admits and recognizes the shame, shares it with another, and is able to take the necessary steps towards real recovery. Your act of sharing can be in a therapy room, a self-help group, with your sponsor, or in group therapy. No matter the setting, it is imperative you find the courage to become vulnerable and find your voice.

In *The Body Keeps the Score*, Dr. van der Kolk writes,

> Feeling listened to and understood changes our physiology; being able to articulate a complex feeling, and having our feelings recognized, lights up our limbic brain and creates an 'aha' moment. As long as you keep secrets and suppress information, you are fundamentally at war with yourself. Hiding your core feelings takes an enormous amount of energy, it zaps your motivation to pursue worthwhile goals, and it leaves you feeling bored and shut down.[139]

Dr. van der Kolk continues,

> unspoken words can be discovered, uttered, and received, [it] is fundamental to healing the isolation of trauma — especially if

---

138   Griffin, 2014
139   van der Kolk, 2014

other people in our lives have ignored or silenced us. Communicating fully is the opposite of being traumatized.[140]

Sharing activates the process of healing emotionally, physically, and on a neurophysiological and neurobiological level. The client's willingness and ability to share their story is of greatest concern to their therapist. In my personal practice, it is crucial that I create a safe, caring environment in which the client can risk vulnerability: telling their story and letting their secrets be made known to ultimately advance toward healing.

It is common, when in the midst of simply sharing your story, to have sudden moments of clarity and insight. Insight is gaining awareness of new knowledge and the identification of a deep, intuitive understanding of yourself, your thoughts and feelings, your behavior, or some combination thereof. These moments of insight are like turning on a light inside of a dark, musty cellar only to find unrealized valuables. Insight is the catalyst that fosters change.

Bruno's story is a short illustration of insight. Once, when Bruno was 18 and living in New York, many of his friends were preparing to go out for the evening. When he turned his key in the ignition, he heard the click of a dead battery. Getting out his jumper cables, he prepared to charge the battery, but, without any previous experience, he realized that he didn't truly know where to begin. Thankfully, his friends were able to help. Hector was young, exceptionally handsome, muscular, and overly popular with the ladies. Immediately, Hector volunteered to take the cable, hook everything up, and save the day. Instead of being thankful for his assistance, though, Bruno felt a deep sense of anger and resentment rise within him toward Hector; its force was shocking even to him. As Hector worked, Bruno asked himself, "What is going on with me?

---

140   van der Kolk, 2014

Why do I feel anger and resentment at him for being so helpful?" He examined the source of these feelings. Bruno suddenly understood that his anger was towards his father for not teaching him how to charge a dead car battery. Now he was helplessly standing beside his car as his muscular, popular friend was fixing the situation, causing him to feel inadequate. It took a few minutes, but Bruno was able to determine the origin of his irrational emotion and worked to calm his emotions, allowing his anger to remain hidden until it finally dissipated. After his self-discovery, he was able to express a sincere appreciation to Hector.

Bruno has drawn on this insightful experience many times when issues of gender role conflict have emerged. There have been moments in his life in which he hasn't had the knowledge base to do something that he felt like a "real man" should be able to do. He now recognizes his underlying belief that he should have been taught these skills. Without this insight, anger can well up within him and can be projected onto others. Now, Bruno is consciously aware of these situations and recognizes that they are a trigger for his underlying anger and can now talk himself through these moments and bring clarity to his mind and the situation. He now accepts himself as fully male and no longer believes that not knowing how to do certain tasks affects his degree of manliness.

Insight can be fostered through many ways, especially through therapy sessions. It is not uncommon for issues to be intergenerational, and because of this, I often conduct *a family genogram*, going back at least three generations. A genogram can quickly illuminate patterns within a family system. To do this, clients supply the name and age of their ancestors, mark if they are dead or living, and give a full description of each individual's personality — the memories that stand out most about this person, any addictive behaviors that are known, and any form of abuse the person endured or afflicted. Once the genogram is completed, it is easier to recognize familial patterns. For example, a great-grandfather may have abandoned his young children after having an affair, the grandfather followed the same pattern, the client's father did as well, and now the young male client sits in my office, hoping to not repeat the same destructive patterns of his forefathers.

The next tool for building insight is often a *life timeline*, with which clients examine their life, beginning with early development, to identify the attachment types they experienced with their caregivers. Together with the patient, we discuss Pia Melody's five areas of a child's nature: children are valuable, vulnerable, imperfect, dependent, and immature. As the timeline progresses, I ask the individual to identify significant memories and events, memories of abuse and/or neglect, sexual development, relationships, hurts, and triumphs. Again, this process typically fosters great insight. It also provides me, as the therapist, an opportunity to draw conclusions and test hypotheses based on the collaborative work of the genogram and the timeline.

Many questions are posed throughout the therapeutic process, and it is essential for patients to examine where boundary violations have occurred, as well as the response to these significant events. We have three modes of responding in the face of trauma: fight, flight, or freeze. I pose questions like these to my patients: *How did you respond? What was the experience like? What are you continuing to experience as a result of your response? Where do you feel this in your body?*

Not all important insights and points of understanding happen inside the therapy room. Having clients read books as an ancillary to therapy can assist in the recovery time and degree of healing a person can experience. I am a strong believer that the more a person can make sense and meaning of their experience, the greater the healing. Therefore, I often suggest to individuals that it will help to read books related to their situation. I often suggest the client read Dr. Peter Levine's book, *Waking the Tiger*, to understand the importance of identifying trauma reactions within the body. I also recommend Dr. Bessel van der Kolk's book, *The Body Keeps the Score*, to understand how the body and brain process trauma, how these memories are stored, and various techniques one can employ to become "unstuck" from trauma, or "to get back on-line", in the words of Dr. van der Kolk. These ancillary forms of information can assist the client, and the therapist, in understanding the idiosyncratic nature of each person's experience, trauma, and necessary components of recovery.

As a therapist, I am looking for patterns, especially if situations developed early in life from either attachment issues or trauma. I attempt to take the pieces of a person's story and put the puzzle together, creating a unique mosaic of their life. I then can help my patients put these pieces together with insight, understanding, and meaning. With the objective help of a therapist, one can begin seeing other realities instead of the one that they have lived. They are now more equipped to see their own life objectively, making sense of their experience and behavior. Insight can be powerful to the change process.

Throughout therapy, I am acutely listening for the presence of shame and where it affects the individual. I listen closely for experienced traumas, and specifically, how these traumas bred shame. Because shame is an internal type of mental scrutiny, it leads to self-disparaging behaviors. If this process is reoccurring, the shame becomes toxic shame. Similarly, if trauma occurs repeatedly, it often leads to a complex trauma. As a therapist, my role is to help patients understand how toxic shame and complex trauma are working together to destroy the self through the development of unhealthy thought, feeling, and behavior patterns.

Change

Change can happen! You are ready for change when you have unpacked your personal baggage and pilfered through the contents, making sense of its meaning. Change begins by learning how to accept yourself as you are —flaws, gifts, talents, and all. Therapy is similar to completing Step 4 and 5 of A.A. Step 4 reads, "Made a searching and fearless moral inventory of ourselves." Step 5 reads, "Admitted to God, to ourselves, and to another human being the exact nature of our wrongs." Granted, abuse and trauma are not "our" wrongdoings, but it is important to examine loss, abandonment, and fear and admit these to the self and to someone else. Once we have acknowledged all the aspects of who we are, we can learn to accept the self and all the unique positive and negative characteristics that make up our whole. We all have a story; we all have hurts and pains from the past; we all possess the power of choice, not always making good decisions for ourselves; and we all have character flaws. A person in the change stage is learning to accept him- or herself with their strengths and weaknesses. This involves re-thinking and re-working your self-concept, beginning with self-acceptance and self-esteem.

Self-acceptance and self-esteem are not the same concepts. Self-esteem refers to the positive feelings we have about the parts of ourselves that we see as good. Self-acceptance, however, is much broader. We approach self-acceptance in an unconditional manner, accepting ourselves globally, including both our strengths and weaknesses. Through self-acceptance, we see ourselves as a work in progress and accept that some parts are better developed than others. It allows us to recognize and acknowledge our hurts, habits, and hang-ups, as well as our strengths.

The basis for the self-acceptance process comes from witnessing the ability of our primary caregivers to accept us, allowing us to have value, vulnerability, imperfection, dependence, and to be spontaneous without shame. In early childhood, we do not possess the ability to see our-selves separately from our parents. As we progress through the matura-tion process, we gain a sense of self. How a caregiver has modeled and demonstrated self-acceptance is our first introduction to the process. If, through this process, there were conditions of 'earning' worth, learning to fully accept oneself may be a life-long challenge. Parents and primary caregivers provide us with a model of caring and parenting that later becomes our own self-care and self-parenting.

Pia Melody writes, "Healthy self-esteem is the internal experience of one's own preciousness and value as a person."[141] Moving into a place of healthy mental health means reformulating your ideals of you! The more a person accepts who they are, the less what others think of them mat-ters. Negative emotions such as shame and self-doubt can be overcome through self-acceptance.

Although therapy is not about finding and placing blame, at times, those who have traumatized us must be identified and confronted. If an individual has experienced abuse, neglect, bullying, and other harmful treatments, a confrontation may be warranted; however, it must be done constructively for closure and healing. One must carefully examine who and how to confront. A verbal or physical attack on someone who has hurt you will not bring closure. Confrontation must be planned out and timed accordingly. A therapist can help you identify if it is appropriate to confront the person and the likelihood of any resulting harm or fur-ther damage.

A confrontation is not intended to get revenge. The patient should care-fully work with a therapist to identify his or her goals for the confron-tation: it is typically used as an intervention to help resolve and bring

141   Melody, 1989

closure to past trauma. If confronting a person has the potential of re-traumatizing the individual, the therapist should discourage the event. Confrontations must be planned to help resolve unfinished issues and return the shame to the person to whom it belongs. One cannot initiate a confrontation hoping to hear specific words or see specific behaviors from the antagonist; often, they will not give you what you want. One cannot anticipate an admission of wrongdoing or an apology. A confrontation is used to allow an individual who has been hurt to find their voice, share their secret, speak their truth, acknowledge what has happened, and to give the shame back to the source so the patient can let go of the carried, toxic shame.

Some individuals will feel the need to forgive the person who wronged them in order to let go of the anger and shame they have carried. If forgiveness is possible, it is encouraged; however, it is important to remember that forgiveness does not mean reconciliation. Forgiveness does not require entering back into a relationship with the person who hurt them. Often, revitalizing such a relationship would be an unhealthy choice. Part of the confrontation is the re-establishment of boundaries with this person, and sometimes those boundaries include severing contact with them.

Another step in the change process is deciding if you had any responsibility for the events that transpired. Please note, any abuse, whether physical, sexual, verbal, or neglect, is never a child's fault — they are never to blame for their own abuse. It is the adult's responsibility to protect them. At times, individuals will blame themselves for abuse, especially in cases of sexual abuse.

Brent, a middle-aged patient, is just now coming to terms with his history of sexual abuse. For many years, he has blamed himself for the sexual abuse he endured from his female babysitter. At 11 years old,

Brent watched an R-rated and sexually explicit movie with his 28-year-old babysitter. Brent became uncomfortable during the movie and had a difficult time hiding his erection from the woman. She assured him that how his body was responding was natural and asked if he had any questions. Brent decided to ask a few questions about sex. The babysitter answered the questions, and suggested that they try some of the things that they saw on TV when the movie ended. Brent dreaded the movie coming to an end and was feeling a tornado of different emotions. Though he knew his body was responding enjoyably to what he was seeing on the screen, he also was very apprehensive about what was to come with the babysitter at the end of the film. After the movie, he and the babysitter experimented sexually, which led to several other sexual encounters over the next few years, most of which were initiated by the older babysitter. Over time, Brent became an angry teenage boy. In his adult years, he has had a string of unhealthy relationships in which he raged at the women, and was unable to maintain a long-term, loving relationship. During therapy, Brent blames himself for the abuse and holds himself responsible for getting an erection, asking sexual questions, and for allowing his babysitter to "use" him. Helping Brent understand that his sexual abuse was not his fault was a huge step in the healing and change process.

In some cases, an individual may be able to determine they did have some responsibility for the event, or even have replicated the hurt done to them. Sometimes, to gain control over feelings of loss and abandonment, individuals will repeat the pattern of abuse that they endured. Psychodynamic theory has termed this as "identification with the aggressor". Instead of facing the hurt and loss of control one might feel from abusive events, a person will identify with their aggressor and traumatize others in an effort to gain back the feeling of power and control that was originally taken from them. It is important for these individuals to own their behavior and the hurt that they have caused others. Self-examination to determine the degree of your responsibility is an important part of the healing process.

If appropriate, part of your change process may be making amends with those you may have harmed. Again, I refer to the 12 Steps for guidance in this process. Step 8 reads, "Made a list of all persons we had harmed, and became willing to make amends to them all." Step 9 reads, "Made direct amends to such people wherever possible, except when to do so would injure them or others". The therapist can help decide if making amends is appropriate. However, whether it is possible to make amends or not, it is equally important that the individual find a way to resolve and forgive themself for the wrongs they committed.

When making amends with a person is impossible, there are many other symbolic ways to work on resolving and forgiving one's behavior. For instance, a therapist may ask the individual to write letters of responsibility and read them aloud during their session to help process the associated feelings. If you have the opportunity to be in group therapy, the therapist may ask you to pick out another group member to represent the other person while you read your letter or process the event. Whatever therapeutic method is chosen, it is important that the individual finds a path to self-forgiveness. The freedom that comes through this process can be the impetus for change.

CONCLUSION

No matter what has happened in the past or what steps have been taken to resolve the issues, it is necessary to understand that your past does not dictate your future. A common saying in the field of psychology is, "past behavior predicts future behavior". Though this is often true, if a person has taken steps of healing through therapy or their own work (like with the 12 steps program), the past does not *have* to predict the future. Change is a conscious process and decision to do things differently. The decision to do things differently changes the brain's reaction — what was once an automatic reaction can be altered and morphed into healthy thoughts and behaviors. It involves taking charge of your life's decisions and living a life founded in healthy emotions and cognitions instead of the distortions of the past.

In order for change to occur, a person may have to remind him or herself to stay in the present. They may have to inwardly say, "This is not my past: this is my present and I have choices that I can make". Just as forgiveness is not forgetting, deciding to resolve your past does not mean it will not again surface, tempting you to yield to emotional and misguided behaviors and thought patterns. When it does, it must be recognized, and you must be able to personally counsel yourself through the emotions or seek outside help. In an effort to make this process most successful, it can be tremendously beneficial to develop a list of self-statements and behaviors that help you to center yourself, maintaining control of your decisions. Developing this kind of mindfulness is a helpful way to monitor emotional states and drives. These self-introspective, therapeutic processes can assist in objective situation examination; they allow the individual to look at the facts and determine if their past may be adding subjectivity to the true situation.

Developing emotional insight helps the individual formulate new mental boundaries. Thoughts may need to be compartmentalized as one recalls that the situation is over and resolved, allowing conscious and deliberate decision to occur. Still, emotional responses can be erratic and irrationally triggered, seemingly appearing out of nowhere. When this occurs, it is important to work toward acknowledging the emotion for what it truly is, examine its source, and move on toward a healthier experience.

Implementing change not only happens for the individual, but once self-improvement begins, they will likely see positive changes in their relationships. The insight gained allows them to be conscious of their current relationships and to avoid viewing them through the subjective and misguided filter of past, problematic beliefs.

In some areas, you will have to make a conscious choice to change. Decide, within your heart and mind, that you are going to allow yourself to trust again. Building trust can be difficult; you may have to tell yourself every day that you are going to make the choice and take the chance to trust someone.

The biggest area of change is the process of defining new behaviors. After establishing and recognizing them, you can now change the old patterns and replace them with healthier behaviors. Don't be alarmed if you have to tell yourself, "NO" to certain feelings, thoughts, or behaviors. By consciously letting go of problematic behaviors, you have the opportunity to invite new ones into your repertoire. Remember, you are allowed to be imperfect and still be loveable; you are permitted to make mistakes and be granted forgiveness; you are free to feel, expressing those feelings openly, honestly, and safely.

I have attempted to walk you through the process of dismantling toxic shame and complex trauma by using both Ben's specific story and those of some of my other clients. I have outlined how an individual should be parented to best help them develop into a healthy functional adult. When this process goes awry as a result of unhealthy attachment, abuse, or neglect by caregivers, a growth process begins that moves the individual away from proper psychological health. The individual experiences trauma events that develop into shame, which in turn, leads to toxic shame. Repeated occurrences of events and toxic shame leads to complex trauma, and this sequence culminates in the repetition of unhealthy behavioral patterns, such as seeking relief through substances or distraction behaviors. Or, the individual can find strength to recover from their painful past, finding their own map toward mental health, either on their own, through mentorship with a healthy person, or through the change process of professional therapy.

I hope this book has been helpful in understanding the development and transition of trauma, gender identity development, gender role conflict, shame, toxic shame, complex trauma, and unhealthy behaviors. I also hope you have found useful methods and direction within these pages to overcome these difficult challenges. Wherever you are on your journey, I wish all of you *Hope, Clarity, Healing, and Change.*

BIBLIOGRAPHY

Adrian, F. "Affuluenza: The Psychology of Wealth: Is It True That the Pursuit of Acquisition of Wealth Leads to Unhappiness?" *Psychologytoday.com*, 28 Aug. 2014, www.psychologytoday.com/blog/sideways-view/201408/affluenza-the-psychology-wealth.

"Alcoholics Anonymous (AA), the 12-Step Program for Alcoholism Recovery." *Alcohol.org*, www.alcohol.org/alcoholics-anonymous/.

Allan, J. A. "The Purity of His Maleness: Masculinity in Popular Romance Novels." *The Journal of Men's Studies*, vol. 24, 2016, pp. 24–41, doi.org/10.1177/1060826515624382.

American Psychiatric Association. *Diagnostic and Statistical Manual of Mental Disorders*, 5th ed., American Psychiatric Publishing, 2013.

Arrindell, W. A., et al. "Biological Sex, Sex Role Orientation, Masculine Sex Role Stress, Dissimulation and Self-Reported Fears." *Advances in Behavior Research and Therapy*, vol. 15, no. 2, 1993, pp. 103–146.

Bem, S. L. "Gender Schema Theory: A Cognitive Account of Sex Typing." *Psychological Review*, vol. 88, no. 4, 1981, pp. 354–364.

Bem, S. L. "Gender Schema Theory and Its Implications for Child Development: Raising Gender Schematic Children in a Gender Schematic Society." *The Psychology of Women*. Edited by M. R. Walsh, Yale University Press, 1987, pp. 226–245.

Bem, S. L. *The Lens of Gender*, Yale University Press, 1993.

Berk, L. *Child Development*, 5th ed., Allyn & Bacon, 2000.

Black, C. *Changing Course: Healing from Loss, Abandonment, and Fear.* Hazelden Publishing, 1993.

Blakemore, J. "Children's Beliefs about Violating Gender Norms: Boys Shouldn't Look like Girls, and Girls Shouldn't Act like Boys." *Sex Roles*, vol. 48, no. 9-10, 2003, pp. 411–419.

Blazing, C., et al. "The Relationship between Masculinity Ideology, Loneliness, and Separation-Individuation Difficulties." *Journal of Men's Studies*, vol. 15, no. 1, 2007, pp. 101–109.

Borden, C., and K. Obsatz. "Journeyman." MirrorMan Films, 2007.

Boundless Psychology. *Development of Gender Identity.* 6 Jan. 2016, www.boundless.com/psychology/textbooks/boundless-psychology-textbook/gender-and-sexuality-15/gender-414/development-of-gender-identity-297-12832/.

Boyle, E., and S. Brayton. "Aging Masculinities and 'Muscle Work' in Hollywood Action Film: An Analysis of the Expendables." *Men and Masculinities*, vol. 15, no. 5, 2012, pp. 468–485.

Brown, J. A. "The Tortures of Mel Gibson: Masochism and the Sexy Male Body." *Men and Masculinities*, vol. 5, 2002, pp. 123–143., doi:10.1177/1097184X02005002001.

Bruno, C. *Hungry Man: Hungry Father. Restoration Project [Web Log]*, 18 Feb. 2013, restorationproject.net/hungry-man-father-hunger/.

"Bullying and Suicide." Bullying Statistics, 7 July 2015, www.bullyingstatistics.org/content/bullying-and-suicide.html.

"Bullying and Suicide. A Review." *International Journal of Adolescent Medical Health*, vol. 20, no. 2, pp. 133–154., Accessed 2008.

Carnes, P. *The Betrayal Bond: Breaking Free of Exploitive Relationship*, Health Communications, Inc., 1997.

Courtenay, W. H. "Constructions of Masculinity and Their Influence on Men's Well-Being. A Theory of Gender and Health." *Social Science & Medicine*, vol. 50, no. 10, pp. 1385–1401.

Covington, S, et al. *A Man's Workbook: A Program for Treating Addiction*, 1st ed., Jossey-Bass A. Wiley Imprint, 2011.

Crib, R. *The Grim Evidence That Men Have Fallen behind Women.* 26 Dec. 2012, www.thestar.com/life/2011/11/25/rob_cribb_the_grim_evidence_that_men_fallen_behind_women.html.

Drummond, M., and C. Drummond. "It's All about the Six-Pack: Boy's Bodies in Contemporary Western Culture." *Journal of Child Health Care*, vol. 19, no. 4, 16 June 2014, pp. 423–431, journals.sagepub.com/doi/abs/10.1177/1367493514538128.

Dutton, D. G., et al. "The Role of Shame and Guilt in the Intergenerational Transmission of Abusiveness." *Violence & Victims*, vol. 10, no. 2, 1995, pp. 121–131.

Eagles, A. H., and V. J. Eisler. "Gender Stereotypes Stem from the Distribution of Women and Men into Social Roles." *Journal of Personality and Social Psychology*, vol. 46, no. 4, 1984, pp. 735–754.

Eagley, A. H., and V. J. Steffen. "Gender Stereotypes Stem from the Distribution of Women and Men into Social Roles." *Journal of Personality and Social Psychology*, vol. 46, no. 4, Apr. 1984, pp. 735–754, dx.doi.org/10.1037/0022-3514.46.4.735.

Efthim, P. W., et al. "Gender Role Stress in Relation to Shame, Guilt, and Externalization." *Journal of Counseling & Development*, vol. 79, no. 4, 2001, pp. 430–438.

Eisenberg, N. "Emotions, Regulation & Moral Development." *Annual Review of Psychology*, vol. 51, 2000, pp. 665–697.

Eisler, R. M., and J. R. Skidmore. "Masculine Gender Role Stress: Scale Development and Component Factors in the Appraisal of Stressful Situations." *Behavior Modification*, vol. 11, no. 2, 1987, pp. 123–136.

Eisler, R. M., and J. A. Blalock. "Masculine Gender Role Stress: Implications for the Assessment of Men." *Clinical Psychology Review*, vol. 11, no. 1, 1991, pp. 45–60.

Eisler, R. M. "The Relationship between Masculine Gender Role Stress and Men's Health Risk: The Validation of a Construct." *A New Psychology of Men*, edited by R. F. Levant and W. S. Pollack, Basic, New York, NY, 1995, pp. 207–255.

Evans, L., and K. Davies. "No Sissy Boys Here: A Content Analysis of the Representation in Elementary School Reading Text Books." *Sex Roles*, vol. 42, no. 3-4, 2000, pp. 255–270.

Fisch, H. *The New Naked: The Ultimate Sex Education for Grown Ups.* Sourcebooks, Inc, 2014.

Fitzgibbons, R. "The Origins and Healing of Homosexual Attractions." *CatholicCulture.org*, 2010, www.catholicculture.org/culture/library/view. cfm?id=3112.

Ford, E. E. "Shame and Empathy: Relational Factors Affecting the Intergenerational Transmission of Family Violence." ProQuest Dissertation & Thesis Global (251681313), 2001.

Gallagher, A. M., and J. C. Kaufman, editors. *Gener Differences in Mathematics: An Integrative Psychological Approach.* Cambridge University Press, 2005.

Gilkerson, L. "Get the Latest Pornography Statistics." *Covenant Eyes*, 19 Feb. 2013, www.covenanteyes.com/2013/02/19/ pornography-statistics/.

Gill, R., et al. "A Genealogical Approach to Idealized Male Body Imagery." *Paragraph*, vol. 26, no. 1/2, 2003, pp. 187–197.

Gillespie, B. M., and R. M. Eisler. "Development of the Feminine Gender Role Stress Scale. A Cognitive-Behavioral Measure of Stress, Appraisal, and Coping for Women." *Behavior Modification*, vol. 16, no. 3, 1 July 1992, pp. 426–438., doi.org/10.1177/01454455920163008.

Goffman, E. *Stigma: Notes on the Management of Spoiled Identity.* Prentice-Hall, 1963.

Griffin, D. *A Man's Way through Relationships: Learning to Love and Be Loved.* Central Recovery Press, 2014.

Hartford, T. C., et al. "Personality Correlates of Masculinity-Femininity." *Psychological Reports*, vol. 21, no. 3, pp. 881–884.

Herbenick, D., et al. "Erect Penile Length and Circumference Dimensions of 1,661 Sexually Active Men in the United States." *The Journal of Sexual Medicine*, vol. 11, no. 1, 2014, pp. 93–101, doi:10.1111/jsm.12244.

Herzog, J. *Father Hunger: Exploitations with Adults and Children*. Routledge, N.Y., 2014.

Herzog, J. "On Father Hunger: The Father's Role in the Modulation of Aggressive Drive and Fantasy." *Father and Child*, edited by S. Cath, et al., Little, Brown and Company, pp. 163–174.

Hoffman, C., and N. Hurst. "Gender Stereotypes: Perception or Rationalization." *Journal of Personality and Social Psychology*, vol. 58, no. 2, Feb. 1990, pp. 197–208, dx.doi.org/10.1037/0022-3514.58.2.197.

Houston, A C, et al. "Sex Typing." *Handbook of Child Psychology: Socialization, Personality and Social Development*, vol. 4, Wiley, New York, NY, 1983, pp. 387–467.

"Internet Statistics." *GuardChild: Protecting Children in the Digital Age*, www.guardchild.com/statistics/.

Jarvis, P. "Born to Play: The Bicultural Roots of Rough and Tumble Play, and It Impact upon Young Children's Learning and Development." *Play and Learning in the Early Years*, edited by P. Broadhead, et al., Sage, 2010, pp. 387–467.

Kalbfleisch, P. J., and M. J. Cody, editors. *Gender, Power, and Communication in Human Relationships*. Lawrence Erlbaum Associates, 1995.

Kim, Y. S., and B. Levental. "Bullying & Suicide. A Review." *International Journal of Adolescent Medical Health*, vol. 20, no. 2, 2008, pp. 133–154.

Kimmel, M. S., and M. Messner. *Men's Lives*. Macmillan, 1989.

Kortsch, G. *Fatherless Women: What Happens to the Adult Woman Who Was Raised without Her Father? [Web Log Comment]*. 0AD, www. trans4mind.com/counterpoint/index-happiness-wellbeing/kortsch4. shtml.

Krugman, S. "Male Development and the Transformation of Shame." *A New Psychology of Men*, edited by W. S. Pollack and R. F. Levant, Basic Books, 1995, pp. 91–126.

Kruk, E. *Father Absence, Father Deficit, Father Hunger: The Vital Importance of Paternal Presence in Children's Lives*. 23 May 2012, www. psychologytoday.com/blog/co-parenting-after-divorce/201205/ father-absence-father-deficit-fasther-hunger.

Kubany, E. S., and S. B. Watson. "Guilt: Elaboration of a Multidimensional Model." *Psychological Record*, vol. 53, no. 1, 2003, pp. 51–90.

Lansky, M. R. *Fathers Who Fail: Shame and Psychopathy in Family System*. Analytic Press, 1992.

Levant, R. F. "Toward the Reconstruction of Masculinity." *Journal of Family Psychology*, vol. 5, no. 3-4, 1992, pp. 379–402.

Levant, R. F., et al. "The Male Role: An Investigation of Norms and Stereotypes." *Journal of Mental Health Counseling*, vol. 14, no. 3, 1992, pp. 325–337.

Levant, R. F., et al. "Male Role Norms Inventory-Short Form (MRNI-SF): Development, Confirmatory Factor Analytic Investigation of Structure, and Measurement Invariance across Gender." *Journal of Counseling Psychology*, vol. 60, no. 2, 2013, pp. 228–238.

Lewis, H. B. *Shame and Guilt in Neurosis*. International Universities Press, 1971.

Lewis, M. *Shame: The Exposed Self.* The Free Press, 1995.

Lima, A. A., et al. "The Impact of Tonic Immobility Reaction on the Prognosis of Post-Traumatic Stress Disorder." *Journal of Psychiatry*, vol. 44, no. 4, 2010, pp. 224–228.

Maccoby, E. E., and R. G. D'Andrade. *The Development of Sex Differences*. Vol. 5, Stanford University Press, 1966.

Mahalik, J. R., et al. "Development of the Conformity to Masculine Norms Inventory." *Psychology of Men and Masculinity*, vol. 4, no. 1, 2003, pp. 3–25.

Martin, C. L., and D. Ruble. "Children's Search for Gender Cues Cognitive Perspectives on Gender Development." *Current Directions in Physiological Science*, vol. 13, no. 2, 2004, pp. 67–70.

Meeker, M. *Strong Father, Strong Daughters: 10 Secrets Every Father Should Know*. Regency Publishing, 2016.

Mellen, H. S. "Rough-and-Tumble between Parents and Children and Children's Social Competence." *Dissertation AbstractsInternational*, vol. 63, 2002, p. 1588.

Melody, P. *Facing Codependency: What It Is, Where It Comes from, How It Sabotages Our Lives*. Harper Collins Publishers, Inc., 1989.

"Men: A Different Depression." *American Psychological Association*, 14 July 2005, www.apa.org/research/action/men.aspx.

Miharia, A. "There Are Extreme Tests Men Have to Pass to Become Pornstars. Its Way Harder than You Thought." *Scoopwhoop.com*, 24 July 2017, www.scoopwhoop.com/extreme-tests-for-men--to-become-pornstars/#.0e0dnejfk.

Modleski, T. *Loving with a Vengeance: Mass-Produced Fantasies for Women*, 2nd ed. Routledge, 2008.

Morrison, A. P. *Shame: The Underside of Narcissism*. Routledge, 1989.

Mosher, D. L., and M. Sirkin. "Measuring Macho Personality Constellation." *Journal of Research in Personality*, vol. 18, no. 2, pp. 150–163, doi:10.1016/0092-6566(84)90026-6.

Newman, P., and B. Newman. *Development through Life: A Psychosocial Approach*. Cengage Learning, 2015.

O'Neil, J., et al. "Fifteen Years of Theory and Research on Men's Gender Role Conflict." *A New Psychology of Men*, edited by R. L. Levant and W. S. Pollack, Basic Books, 1995, pp. 164–206.

O'Neil, J. "Summarizing 25 Years of Research on Men's Gender Role Conflict Using the Gender Role Conflict Scale; New Research Paradigms and Clinical Implications." *The Counseling Psychologist*, vol. 38, no. 3, 2008, pp. 358–445.

Ora, C. *9 Critical Skills You Should Have to Become a Male Porn Actor*. 25 Oct. 2016, onedio.co/content/9-critical-skills-you-should-have-to-become-a-male-porn-actor-12361.

Pederson, E. L., and D. L. Vogel. "Male Gender Role Conflict and Willingness to Seek Counseling: Testing a Mediation Model on College-Aged Men." *Journal of Counseling Psychology*, vol. 54, 2007, pp. 373–384., dx.doi.org/10.1037/0022-0167.54.4.373.

Pleck, J. *The Myth of Masculinity.* M.I.T. Press, 1981.

Pleck, J. H. "The Gender Role Strain Paradigm." *A New Psychology of Men*, edited by R. F. Levant and W. S. Pollack, Basic Books, 1995, pp. 11–32.

Poe, M. "The Other Gender Gap." *The Atlantic Monthly*, 2004, p. 137.

Pollack, W. *Real Boys: Rescuing Our Boys from the Myths of Boyhood.* Random House, 1998.

Pollack, W. S., and R. F. Levant. *New Psychotherapy for Men.* Wiley, 1998.

Pollack, W. S. "The Sacrifice of Isaac: A New Psychology of Boys and Men." *Society for the Psychological Study of Men and Masculinity Bulletin*, vol. 4, 1999, pp. 7–14.

Pollack, W. S. "The 'War' for Boys: Hearing 'Real Boys' Voices, Healing Their Pain." *Professional Psychology: Research and Practice*, vol. 37, no. 2, 2006, pp. 190–195.

"Prevention of Suicidal Behaviors: A Task for All." *World Health Organization*, 2018, www.who.int/mental_health/prevention/suicide/background/en/.

Radway, J. *Reading the Romance: Women, Patriarchy, and Popular Literature.* The University of North Carolina Press, 2009.

Stern, P., director. *Raising Cain: Boys in Focus [Motion Picture].* United States: National Geographic Television, 2006.

Raley, S., and S. Bianchi. "Sons, Daughters, & Family Process: Does Gender of Children Matter?" *Annual Reviews Sociology*, vol. 32, 2006, pp. 401–421.

"Relevant Research and Article about the Studies." *Yourbrainonporn. com*, Your Brain on Porn, www.yourbrainonporn.com.

Rizzuto, A. "Shame in Psychoanalysis. The Function of Unconscious Fantasies." *Shame and Sexuality: Psychoanalysis and Usual Culture*, edited by C. Pataczkowska and I. Ward, Routledge, 2008, pp. 53–73.

Rohr, R., and A. Schulte. "Naming the ‚Father Hunger'." *St. James Community of Faith*, Oct. 1990, http://www.stjamesstraford.com/files/ Men's%ministry documents/Father-Hunger[1].pdf.

Ropelato, J. "Internet Pornography Statistics." *Internet Pornography Statistics - Top Ten Reviews*, 28 Mar. 2014, www.ministryoftruth. me.uk/wp-content/uploads/2014/03/IFR2013.pdf.

Ruble, D. N. "Sex Role Development." *Developmental Psychology: An Advanced Textbook (2nd Ed)*, edited by M. H. Barnstein and M. E. Lamb, Erlbaum, 1988.

Ruble, D., and C. Martin. "Children's Search for Gender Cues Cognitive Perspectives on Gender Development." *Current Directions in Physiological Science*, vol. 13, no. 2, 2004, pp. 67–70.

Schalkwijk, F. "Shame in Psychotherapy." *European Federation for Psychotherapy Review*, 2008.

Scott, E. *Hooray! Target Is Making Its Toy Aisles Gender Neutral.* 2015, metro.co.uk/2015/11/hooray-target-is-making-its-toe-aisles-gender-neutral-5338127/#ixzz41Q4q28Ah.

Scrooge, W. *Intergenerational Aspects of Shame - The Legacy of the Greatest Generation.* 24 Sept. 2013, winstonscrooge.wordpress. com/2013/09/24/intergenerational-aspects-of-shame-the-legacy-of-the-greatest-generation/.

Secunda, V. *Women and Their Fathers: The Sexual and Romantic Impact of the First Man in Your Life.* Delta, 1993.

Sengezer, M., et al. "Accurate Methods for Determining Functional Penile Length in Turkish Young Men." *Annals of Plastic Surgery*, vol. 48, no. 4, 2002, pp. 381–385.

Steiner, B. W., editor. *Gender Dysphoria: Development, Research, and Management.* Plenum Press, 1985.

Stoeken, H. J. P. *Psychoanalytisch Woordenboek.* (3e, Gewijzigdedruk), 2008.

Stopaprd, J. M., and K. J. Paisley. "Masculinity, Femininity, Life Stress, and Depression." *Sex Roles*, vol. 16, no. 9-10, 1987, pp. 489–496.

"Suicide." *National Institute of Mental Health*, May 2018, www.nimh. nih.gov/health/statistics/suicide.shtml.

"Suicide Claims More Lives than War, Murder, and Natural Disasters Combined." *American Foundation for Suicide Prevention*, 2016, www.theovernight.org/index.cfm?fuseaction=cms.page&id=1034.

"Suicide Rate Is up 1.2 Percent According to Most Recent CDC Data (Year 2016)." *American Foundation or Suicide Prevention*, 2 Jan. 2018, afsp.org/suicide-rate-1-8-percent-according-recent-cdc-data-year-2016/.

Tangney, J. P. "Conceptual and Methodological Issues in the Assessment of Shame and Guilt." *Behavior Research and Therapy*, vol. 34, no. 9, 1996, pp. 741–754.

Tangney, J. P. "Moral Affect: The Good, the Bad, and the Ugly." *Journal of Personality and Social Psychology*, vol. 61, no. 4, 1991, pp. 598–607.

Tangney, J. P., et al. "Proneness to Shame, Proneness to Guilt, and Psychopathology." *Journal of Abnormal Psychology*, vol. 101, no. 3, 1992, pp. 469–478.

Tangney, J. P., et al. "Shame into Anger? The Relation of Shame and Guilt to Anger and Self-Reported Aggression." *Journal of Personality and Social Psychology*, vol. 62, no. 4, 1992, pp. 669–675.

Terr, L. *Unchained Memories*. Harper Collins Publishers, Inc., 1994.

The Bible. King James Version. Oxford UP, 1998.

Thompkins, C. D. "The Relationship between Bender Role Conflict and Shame in College Males. (Master's Thesis)." *Youngstown State University*, Youngstown State University, Youngstown, OH, 1999.

Thompkins, C. D., et al. "Gender Role Conflict and Shame in College Men." *Psychology of Men and Masculinity*, vol. 4, no. 1, June 2003, pp. 79–81., dx.doi.org/10.1037/1524-9220.4.1.79.

Van der Kolk, B. *The Body Keeps the Score: Brain, Mind, and Body in the Healing of Trauma*. Penguin Random House, 2014.

Walsh, K., et al. "Resiliency Factors in the Relation between Childhood Sexual Abuse and Adult Sexual Assault in College-Age Women." *Journal of Child Sexual Abuse*, vol. 16, no. 1, 2007, pp. 1–17.

Watkins, P. L., et al. "Psychological and Physiological Correlates of Male Gender Role Stress among Employed Adults." *Behavioral Medicine*, vol. 17, no. 2, 1991, pp. 86–90.

Wessells, H., et al. "Penile Length in the Flaccid and Erect States: Guidelines for Penile Augmentation." *The Journal of Urology*, vol. 156, no. 3, 1996, pp. 995–997.

Witt, S. D. "Parental Influence on Children's Socialization to Gender Rolesl." *Adolescence*, vol. 32, no. Summer, 1997, pp. 253–259.

"What Is Cyberbullying." StopBullying.gov, Department of Health and Human Services, 7 Feb. 2018, www.stopbullying.gov/cyberbullying/what-is-it/index.html.

World Health Organization. www.who.int/.

Zeglin, R. J. "Portrayals of Masculinity in 'Guy Movies': Exploring Viewer-Character Dissonance." *The Journal of Men's Studies*, vol. 24, no. 1, 2016, pp. 42–59, doi:http://dx.doi.org/10.1177/1060826515624390.

Zimbardo, P. G., and N. Duncan. "The Demise of Guys: Why Boys Are Struggling and What We Can Do about It." Amazon Digital Services, 2012.

AUTHOR BIOGRAPHY

D r. Carpenter is a Licensed Psychologist and professor in the field of psychology. He and his spouse, Mary Carpenter, LMSW are the founders of Insight Counseling Services in Rochester, Michigan. Dr. Carpenter has a doctoral degree in Clinical Psychology from the Forest Institute of Professional Psychology; earned a Master of Science in Counseling and Substance Abuse Rehabilitation from Pace University; and has an Associates of Arts in Theological Studies from Kent Christian College.

He has a keen ability to translate academic psychology and sound clinical research into clinical practice and in his writings. He has a broad range of knowledge treating an array of psychological, emotional, and behavioral disorders with extensive study and therapeutic skills in the area of gender role conflict, shame, sexual abuse and trauma, and chemical and behavioral addictions.

Dr. Carpenter is actively involved in his community and has been president of and served on several drug and alcohol prevention programs and has served on numerous academic boards and committees. He enjoys reading, studying, research, music, and spending time with his two children, Dawson and Morgan; his wife, Mary; and his three Cavalier King Charles Spaniels: Louis, Bentley and Camella.